THE
SCOTS
BOOK OF
FOOTBALL

THE SCOTS *BOOK OF* FOOTBALL

WOLFE PUBLISHING LTD

10 Earlham Street   London WC2

SBN 72340141 1
© Wolfe Publishing Ltd. 1969

Printed by Jarrold & Sons, Ltd., Norwich

CONTENTS

CONTENTS *CONTINUED*

Mission Mexico!

by BOBBY BROWN

(Scottish international team manager)

"SCOTLAND FOR MEXICO!" That is the battle slogan I have adopted for the World Cup and I am confident we can fight our way into the finals next summer.

Why am I so optimistic after we have dropped a home point to West Germany? Because the Scottish players have shown that they revel in a situation when their backs are to the wall. Traditionally, we are fighters. Certainly, we've two hard games to come. The first one against the Germans in Hamburg on 8 October and the other against Austria in Vienna on 5 November. Tough ties by all means, but the task is not impossible.

You may remember that during the qualifying stages of the Nations Cup, we beat England at Wembley in 1967 and were ideally placed at the halfway stage of the two-season event. What happened? Scotland flopped against Ireland

Murdoch beats goalkeeper Wolter to score Scotland's only goal—and to gain a vital point—in the match against West Germany at Hampden Park

at Windsor Park and that defeat cost us a place in the knock-out stages. So I agree that the task is difficult.

Nobody appreciates more than I do what an immense advantage we would have had if only Scotland had beaten West Germany at Hampden, but I feel that too little credit was given to the team which, after all, finished runners-up to England in 1966.

In my various spy missions to assess the strength of the German squad, I was impressed by their outstanding method and self-discipline. They will always be hard to beat, but it wasn't until they played at Hampden that Helmut Schoen, the German team manager, was able to field his strongest side which included the Italian League pair, Schnellinger and Haller.

I rate the Germans in the first three in world football and, needless to say, I consider that the winners of our section

Left: *The West Germans under pressure: a shot by Bobby Lennox is brilliantly tipped over the bar by Wolter.* **Above**: *Johnstone's sizzler is saved by substitute goalkeeper Maier*

will do extremely well in Mexico even under conditions that won't suit the Europeans.

It is regrettable that Scotland's plans to tour Mexico in the close season fell through because the host nation found it impossible to fit us into their busy schedule.

The Germans have been very sporting Cup opponents. Their team manager told me that in the event of Scotland qualifying, he will give me a complete dossier on the conditions in Mexico so that we can reap the rewards of their missionary trip. This is a first-class gesture.

The Germans have the advantage over us that their team plays many more internationals and so the players have more opportunities to grow accustomed to each other's style. This was borne out by their teamwork in that game against us. In that match the German team had collected

Scotland versus Cyprus: goalkeeper Alkivades can only sit and stare as Colin Stein's fourth goal goes in

370 caps between them in comparison to the Scottish total of 170. And, while our rivals had played their last ten games inside a year, it had taken Scotland from November, 1966 to April, 1969 to complete the same number of games. These are significant points which emphasise why the Germans are such a well-drilled combination.

West Germany are steeped in World Cup football and they were seeded to qualify in our group. It was our misfortune to be drawn against them and I am sure it is harder to qualify in the Jules Rimet tournament than to play in the finals. The further you go in anything, the better you play.

Anyhow, I reckon we can force a draw in Hamburg—even if two points would be most welcome—and then win in

A mix-up in the Cyprus goalmouth: Gilzean and Bremner (No. 4) go in for an Eddie Gray cross

13

Austria. In the end, goal difference may decide which country wins the section; our 5–0 victory over Cyprus in Nicosia and 8–0 success against them at Hampden could prove to be as valuable as any other results.

If we reach the Prater Stadium needing two points to make Mexico, I'm sure my players will pull out every stop. Past history shows that the two countries have had some stormy tussles and that it isn't exactly a happy hunting ground for Scotland. But we must overcome any feelings of pessimism and go there in search of success.

I shall make a point of watching the Austrians again at the Prater Stadium before our game and, believe me, we respect them after the splendid display they put up in Glasgow where we came from behind to win 2–1.

But the fact remains that we don't deserve to be Mexico-bound unless we are capable of winning in Vienna. Don't forget the Germans won in Austria and the Scots must be able to equal or surpass any achievement of Beckenbauer and his colleagues.

Harking back to our 1–1 draw at Hampden, I was delighted by the attitude of my players as they splashed about in the bath after the game. They were super-confident of holding or beating Germany in October and that outlook won't have changed when the match comes around. Indeed, their unanimous verdict was that in another ten minutes they would have licked the opposition.

We haven't appeared in the World Cup finals since 1958— and that's a long time to be out of the limelight.

You can be sure that the Germans will not be too cocky, although they have that incredible record of never having lost a qualifying match in the global tournament. But they don't talk so much about their efforts against Scotland. For this is the one country they have never managed to beat. I firmly believe there will be no change in these statistics after our match at the Volksparkstadion and that we'll be on our way to Mexico.

A FIRST MINUTE SHOCK...

It's a minute after kick-off and a shock for Celtic as a shot by Allan puts Morton one up in the Scottish Cup semi-final

TREASON!
but I still say this about Scottish football

by PAT CRERAND

(Manchester United's Scottish international wing-half)

FEW COUNTRIES in the world produce as many naturally gifted footballers as are bred in Scotland. Yet if I had to choose a British eleven, I would not select any stars from Scottish clubs. My choices, in fact, would be *Anglos* such as Eddie McCreadie (Chelsea), Billy Bremner (Leeds United) and Denis Law (Manchester United).

Coming from me that statement will probably be regarded as treason in Glasgow, the city in which I was born and where

Celtic and Rangers occupy the throne of Scottish soccer power. But I insist on making the point because I believe that the leading players in Scotland suffer through being in an environment which offers such precious little scope for improvement.

To my mind, no players here—and I include those from Celtic and Rangers—can be considered outstanding as individuals until they have consistently underlined their skills at a more demanding competitive level.

And by this, I mean the English First Division.

Pat Crerand knows Scottish football inside out. Here he is playing for Celtic in the days before he moved to make a big name for himself with Manchester United

When I was with Celtic it was never my intention to join the exodus across the Border. But I became involved in a dispute over a coaching matter with the club, which sparked my transfer to Manchester United in 1965 and marked the turning point of my career.

Today, I can appreciate that had I remained in Scotland I might never have fully realised my potential. Sure, I would have savoured plenty of glory and high financial rewards, for Celtic and Rangers have enjoyed the fruits of European combat year after year, and there seems no possibility of their total domination ending in the future.

At the same time, I would not have experienced the professional satisfaction of seeing my ability blossom on a wider scale—of going as far in the game as was humanly possible.

Don't let anyone try to kid you that the general standard of play in the English First Division is not higher than in the Scottish First Division. It is—and appreciably so. The basic difference is that English soccer is played at a faster pace and the approach to all facets of the game is more professional. It is not that English players can run faster than the Scots but that they have a greater tendency to make the ball do all the work.

Most Scottish players like to hold the ball. They are individualists, which is why so many of them find it difficult to conform to a specific tactical pattern. Of course, one must have players of this type in the game. After all, where would soccer be without the George Bests and Charlie Cookes, the ball-playing geniuses who can produce goals no matter how ruthless and well planned the strategy used against them?

My point is that if *too many* players always want to dwell on the ball this must weaken the effectiveness of the team as a whole. Certainly, as far as forwards are concerned, it is so easy to allow defenders to get back into covering positions through this insistence on holding the platform. The fact is that a pass can travel much faster than a player can run—and it is the improvement in passing, or team-work if you like, as much as revolutionary training methods which has resulted in the increased tempo of play in England.

In my opinion, it is fair to say that Jim Baxter, now back

That's Billy Bremner jumping with joy, and playing for Leeds United. He has every reason to be happy with life. The same goes for Denis Law, an idol with Manchester United fans

with Rangers, is a player who has never really adapted himself to English conditions because of this tendency to want to do too much on the ball. He was rated as a world-class performer with Rangers before he crossed the Border, and his experiences in England provide a classic example of the gulf between the two nations. I have a great admiration for Jim's inborn ability. But, compared with the exploits of other Scots like Billy Bremner of Leeds United, and Dave Mackay, the ex-Spurs star now with Derby County, it is questionable if he can be regarded as having reached the very top of the game.

If it were possible for all Scottish players to appear in English football for a season, or at least to create the type of situation in their own country which exists in England, I am positive that they would all improve greatly. Yet only Celtic and Rangers would "live" here. It would take them at least two seasons to acclimatise to the pace of the game in England, to the superior all-round professionalism, to the mental pressure of facing a tough game each week. Neither of them would enjoy major success as regularly as they do in Scotland.

Liverpool manager Bill Shankly recently put forward the view that no team in the First Division faces an away match nowadays and feels confident of avoiding defeat. How right he is! There is hardly anything to choose between teams at the top of the table and those at the bottom. There are no bad teams. Only good ones—and very good ones. Nowhere else in the world are mistakes so cruelly punished, where 100 per cent fitness and confidence are so vital.

Celtic and Rangers have no more than half a dozen really hard matches each season. All the rest are virtually foregone conclusions. Life is too easy for them. Their players are like fast cars that are rarely out of first gear. I am not overlooking the fact that Celtic were the first British club to win the European Cup, and that even in their current environment they must be ranked as one of the truly great teams of world football. Yet surely the sheer challenge of the game south of the Border would provide the stimulation which would lift them to even greater heights of performance and achievement.

To me, their ability is being wasted in Scotland.

For many years Scottish soccer has wallowed in a false sense of supremacy; spurning modern ideas from other countries in the misguided belief that they have had nothing to learn.

Jock Stein of Celtic has been the first to acknowledge the benefits to be derived from keeping pace with the general development of the game. The result is that he has produced a team which is years in advance of its rivals and which is unlikely ever to lose its grip on success. Admittedly more managers are following Stein's lead and adopting a more professional approach to training and tactics. At international level, in particular, there is thankfully no longer the feeling that Scotland can win matches purely by handing their players a blue jersey.

Sadly, however, Scotland still has a long long way to go to produce the same healthy, invigorating air of competition that exists in England. Too many clubs still make the mistake of selling their best players. Too many fans outside Glasgow forsake their own clubs and support Celtic or Rangers purely on the grounds of religious bigotry.

Only when more teams in Scotland have a real chance of winning titles will this country produce outstanding footballers in the fullest sense of the word.

Life on a shoestring

by JIM WEIR

(Secretary, Stenhousemuir)

IT MUST BE a rare feeling to run a football team and have no financial worries. I haven't experienced it. For my club it is nothing new to count every pound—it would take us over twenty years to collect at home games what Celtic pulled in from their European Cup tie with A.C. Milan in March.

There is no point in feeling envious. Celtic have far greater commitments and Stenhousemuir have learned to exist at their own level.

The struggle for survival has been going on for over forty years at Ochilview and I'd say that we have had more experience than most clubs at keeping our head above water. Certainly, it hasn't been easy, but good budgeting is the answer and we manage not too badly.

Many minor clubs in Central Scotland had to fold up in the mid-twenties when professionalism crept in. It was then that Stenhousemuir launched a supporters' club—not to follow the team in away matches, but to provide the indirect income which has been a life-saver to the club through the years.

At no time have Stenhousemuir paid wages they couldn't afford and this is one of the main reasons why the team has shrugged off periods of crises. I call Stenhousemuir a "community club", which means it is not a limited company. I think only Arbroath and Stranraer fall with us into this category. Anyone can become a member by buying a season ticket which might cost 55 shillings or 45 shillings. We consistently keep around 300 members—some of them businessmen who like to make their contribution without watching the team. Indeed, this is true of most Larbert people. They may not take the trouble to attend matches, but they have done their utmost to keep the club in existence.

It used to be outfits like our own which had to organise dances and sweepstakes to find extra funds. Now even Rangers and Celtic have lotteries and, naturally, their mammoth four-figure prizes had a serious effect on our own development club schemes. So we merged in the sweepstake business with our near neighbours East Stirlingshire and other minor teams to enable us to offer a substantial prize-list and keep our customers happy. From this source we can gain anything from £2,000 to £4,000 each year.

This may sound very little, but it's a fortune to us considering that the club can be run for just over £150 a week. Our players cannot afford Jaguars off their wages, but I believe we get better value per pound from our players than any other team manages to do.

Of course, the money we receive from the pools is most welcome. About eighteen months ago Stenhousemuir opened a social club inside Ochilview, which is proving a lucrative source of income already; I fancy a lot more clubs will have similar establishments alongside their football ground in years to come. There is, too, the transfer market, though you can never depend on players being in demand. The club can sell two players in one season and then experience a famine in profitable deals.

However, we have to obtain money outside the game since our average attendances have dwindled to the 500 mark. Consequently we seldom pay more than the £150 guarantee; neither do we receive over the odds on our away trips in the Second Division.

Stenhousemuir usually operate on a playing staff of fourteen and we recruit almost solely from the Stirlingshire area. The juvenile game is in a healthy state and, while our ground is badly situated geographically from a crowd-pulling viewpoint—fans find it easier to travel to Edinburgh or Glasgow—at least it is such a convenient spot that all the players can train together to foster club spirit.

My own feeling is that it is easier for the small-time teams to keep going now than it was in the fifties. I remember the difficulties around 1956, when the Government claimed one-seventh of a club's income through entertainment tax and when sweepstakes were illegal.

Then things were black for Stenhousemuir and people like us; the lifting of the tax was the first big break and soon afterwards the pools money began to give us fresh income.

Five seasons ago during a big purge for reconstruction Rangers wanted to axe the last five clubs in the Second Division and Stenhousemuir figured on the chopping list. But we got together and used legal brains to thwart that move.

I have been secretary of Stenhousemuir since 1950 but the job almost amounts to being manager, even if my title doesn't say so. Like the players, I'm a part-timer; an electrical engineer by day and a football legislator at night . . . every night!

During my time I have advocated the introduction of

three leagues in Scottish football and I know that the teams running the greatest risk would be those in the lowest grade. However, it is my opinion that it would help clubs to find their real level. Stenhousemuir could afford to have a real go at promotion to the Second Division—and don't forget that under the present set-up we have twice finished third in our division, only narrowly missing a step-up into the top sphere.

We are one of the "poor relations" in the country, but I maintain that an extra division would help all clubs, including those in Europe who have so much difficulty in finding suitable dates.

Whatever the formation, I am convinced that there is room for all the small outfits. Our budget has to be strict, but there are many more illustrious clubs who must wish that they had curbed their spending and kept wages to a lower level in the sixties. Most First Division clubs have to sell one or more players a year to balance the books whereas we cannot afford to rely on this avenue of income.

Stenhousemuir could put up a show against any of the big names and maybe teach a few of them something about money management. The past forty years may have been tough, but the next forty will be no easier.

Scotland's bright young men

There has always been a wealth of talent emerging from Scotland's nursery clubs. Indeed, the future of clubs and international football is invested in today's young players. Here are some of the names that are expected soon to make big news.

John Blackley *(Hibs)*
This red-haired defender missed a few winter months owing to a broken bone in his foot, but he showed in the last three months that he could be an Under-23 cap soon as a cover centre-half. He comes from Falkirk and reads the game well for one with so little experience.

Jim Bone *(Partick Thistle)*
Just out of his teens, this nippy striker stepped out of the Airth Castle Rovers junior team into the First Division and became Thistle's most consistent marksman right away. He chalked up one hat-trick to prove that his positional sense is well above average.

Jim Brown *(Hearts)*
An attacking half-back who lacks only experience. He lives a few minutes' walk from Hearts' ground and preferred his local side to many others. He is learning the hairdressing business to provide for later on—but at 19 his immediate future looks bright.

Nippy striker: Jim Bone

Youth cap: Alfie Conn   *Right temperament:* George Connelly

Alfie Conn *(Rangers)*

Son of a famous father who played at inside-forward for Hearts. Young Alfie, 17, occupies the same position but fulfilled a schoolboy ambition in joining Rangers. He plays in midfield and is regarded as high class material. A Youth cap.

George Connelly *(Celtic)*

On the fringe of becoming a recognised first team player, he made his début against Rangers and showed the right temperament. He was playing junior football in Fife as a schoolboy and became noted for his ball juggling. Over 6 feet. Signed from Tulliallan, he could be a centre-half or midfield man.

Raymond Cormack *(Celtic)*

The Parkhead club spotted him playing in Edinburgh schools football and put him on an S-form. He is attached to the crack Salvesen Boys Club team and it may be a year or two before this brilliant inside-forward breaks through.

Alex Cropley *(Hibs)*
He is a tiny 18-year-old left-winger with the heart of a lion. Giant defenders don't scare this smart forward. Eventually he could become an inside-forward. Alex was the first product of the Hibs Supporters' Club team. He was born in Aldershot.

John Gorman *(Celtic)*
Most Parkhead recruits are from the West, but this stylish left-back comes from Winchburgh, near Edinburgh. He uses the ball well and can play half-back, too. John has been with Celtic for five years and devotes his free time to coaching a local boys' team.

Jim Hamilton *(Aberdeen)*
A Falkirk-born youngster who played minor grade football with Dunipace. He quit Rangers ground staff to join the Dons where he was given a first team chance on the wing. A Youth cap, he should develop into a smart centre-forward.

Smart centre-forward: Jim Hamilton   *Top Scorer:* Joe Harper

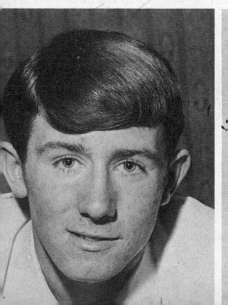

Right-wing wizard: Peter Marinello   *Unfortunate start:* George McKimmie

Joe Harper *(Morton)*

A bustling go-ahead little forward who likes to play centre-forward. He played for Morton, won recognition in Scotland's Youth team and was transferred to Huddersfield. But he didn't settle in England and returned to Morton to be top scorer last season.

Billy McAlpine *(Hearts)*

He became a full-time player this summer at the end of his printing apprenticeship but, already, he has a fair amount of experience. He was asked to step in last season when left-back Arthur Mann was transferred to Manchester City.

Andy McFadden *(St. Mirren)*

He made a big impression in his first season in the Scottish League. Andy starred at centre-half in Saint's promotion year and dealt with the country's best centres in commanding style. A Port Glasgow product, now 20, he would be even better as a full-time professional.

Superb prospect: Hamish McAlpine

Hamish McAlpine *(Dundee United)*
On the evidence of a hurried First Division baptism, the Tannadice reserve goalkeeper looked a superb prospect. He is a local Dundee youngster who signed from the North End Junior club. Hamish will be knocking on the first team door in the coming months.

George McKimmie *(Dunfermline)*

He had an unfortunate start to his senior career last season when he broke a thumb in his first game. But 18-year-old George, who comes from Dundee, played in a European tie in Cyprus some weeks later. He is an inside-forward with a Boys Clubs cap.

Peter Marinello *(Hibs)*

Dozens of clubs wanted the 19-year-old right-wing wizard when he was a schoolboy cap. He was a notable capture for Easter Road. A brilliant dribbler, the slightly built, long-haired youngster made his League début at 17 and experience will make him a star.

Stewart Rennie *(Falkirk)*

He was pitched into the relegation-threatened Brockville team halfway through the season and this goalkeeper matured rapidly in a crisis. He is 19 and just under 6 feet. Rennie belongs to Edinburgh and played with Royston Boys Club.

Derek Robertson *(St. Johnstone)*

A future Scotland goalkeeper who was denied Under-23 recognition last season through cancellations. A Glasgow boy, he is 20 and joined the Perth club from Petershill. He has extremely quick reflexes and should make his representative début shortly.

Ken Watson *(Rangers)*

A youngster in the John Greig mould and built on similar lines. He is a burly teenage wing-half who can turn his feet to defence or attack. Comes from Edinburgh and is yet another product of the Salvesen club. A schoolboy cap.

Tony Wilson *(Aberdeen)*

Another Eddie Turnbull discovery. The Pittodrie boy reckons he has a real capture in this all-action wing-half. Tony belongs to Glasgow and moved north to play with Banks O' Dee. He is 18 and a Youth cap.

MULHERON TO THE RESCUE

Clyde 'keeper Tommy McCulloch looks fearful — but full-back Eddie Mulheron is there to head clear in a match against Celtic

I'm not proud of my behaviour

by COLIN STEIN

For Stein a grim moment of truth. The referee has sent him off the field during a match with Clyde at Ibrox. In utter despair the Rangers' centre-forward sinks to his knees; he cries; he pounds the ground with his fists. For the fourth time in his career he is ordered back to the dressing-room.

...Colin Stein Confesses

"I couldn't sign fast enough..."

ONCE MY PLAYING DAYS are over—and I hope that's a long, long time away—there will be no doubt in my mind as to my most eventful season. I experienced all the ups and downs of football in 1968–69.

Just look at what happened.... Transferred from Hibs to Rangers for £100,000; capped for Scotland in the World Cup; seven goals for my country in four May games; suspended three times for ordering-off offences; and married at the end of it all. Headlines seemed to follow me around everywhere.

But the climax was signing for Rangers. That was my greatest ambition from an early age. I was overjoyed when they took an interest in me and when they tried to persuade Hibs to sell. It was quite a week before the deal went through, for I had turned down the chance to go to Everton a couple of days earlier.

Out of the blue I was told to report to the Caledonian Hotel in Edinburgh to meet Harry Catterick, the Everton manager. He told me all about the tempting terms, the signing-on fee, the great future of the Merseyside club—and how a house would be found for me when I married. It sounded good, but I wanted to talk it over with Linda, then my fiancée. So I asked for a few hours' grace before giving my decision.

The fee was to be about £90,000, of which I would receive 5 per cent (£4,500) over a period of time. And there was that long contract waiting to be signed. . . . Most folk regarded the transfer as a foregone conclusion and I created quite a shock by refusing to move south. Looking back, it was a very rushed decision but I didn't regret it; all the time I was hoping that Rangers would come along with an offer.

I wasn't disappointed. Rangers moved fast and on 31 October I became one of the Light Blues. After lunch at Easter Road I went for a game of snooker with some of my Hibs pals without realising that the two clubs had agreed on terms by telephone. It was only when I went for my train at Waverley Station that reporters told me the transfer was on.

I reached Linlithgow and found a Rangers car waiting there, to whisk me back to Edinburgh. There, manager Davie White and vice-chairman Matt Taylor were sitting in a quiet hotel with the signing-on forms. We discussed wages and prospects—and I couldn't sign fast enough.

Hibs were good to me and it was a wrench leaving my colleagues, but I knew I would benefit both professionally and financially by moving to Ibrox.

That £100,000 tag was a big responsibility to carry around. I thought it would make me a target for defenders, yet I had a pleasant introduction to my playing days with Rangers. My début was at Arbroath; I had the satisfaction of scoring a hat-trick. I was thrilled at having made such a successful

*Stein is an enthusiast, always searching for the chance, always wanting to score goals for Rangers. Here (**above**) the ball is loose and McCulloch, the Clyde goalkeeper, is on the ground. Stein is there, and so is Ferguson (left). This could be a goal. In the air this time (**opposite**) he outjumps Zugazaga, of Atletico Bilbao*

start but I was dead scared about my second game . . . it was against Hibs. And, of course, it was at Ibrox.

Rangers played well, though, and it was another lucky day for me, for I collected another hat-trick. While everyone seemed to be congratulating me, I wondered how the reception would be when I didn't score at all. Anyhow, the next game did not produce that problem, for I had two goals

against Dundalk in the Fairs Cup. However, it wasn't so good in every game; my first disappointment as a Ranger came when we lost 1–0 to St. Mirren at Paisley. Just one goal would have been enough that day, but it didn't come.

The players really got cracking after that nasty shock, and we went over twenty games before our next defeat at Airdrie.

I don't think I'm any better now than I was during my Easter Road days but there are more good players around me so, naturally, more chances come to me. And there is one thing I'm particularly glad about—I don't have to face Ronnie McKinnon any more. I always regarded him as the most formidable centre-half I had to meet. Fortunately, the problem is now resolved for me.

I was still with Hibs when Scotland's manager, Bobby Brown, chose me to play in a friendly match against Denmark in Copenhagen. It was a wonderful honour even if it was not a competitive match. Although we won 1–0, I did not perform too well. Happily, I didn't have to wait long for another chance to prove myself. I played in the World Cup tie against Cyprus in Nicosia and Scotland played well in bad conditions. We won 5–0.

A five-week suspension gave me no chance of turning out against West Germany in the spring but I'll be trying all I know to make the return game in October, having enjoyed my four international appearances in May.

I am not proud of my behaviour last season, having been ordered off when I was playing for Hibs against Raith Rovers. I was ordered off again in matches against Kilmarnock and Clyde.

I have been banned for about nine weeks as a Rangers player and I must make sure it doesn't happen again: It is not fair to the rest of my colleagues.

After a little more than half a season with Rangers, I am convinced there is no greater club. They have shown immense faith in my ability; I hope to repay the club officials by helping them to a good share of the honours in the coming years.

The strange point about my career is that I became a centre-forward almost by accident. I was a left-back with

Armadale Thistle and suddenly I was switched to centre-forward.

We played Penicuik Athletic in a Cup final at Easter Road and I scored three goals with Hibs manager Bob Shankly looking on. Partick Thistle wanted me to sign, too, but I preferred Hibs and nobody considered that I was a full-back any longer.

It's just another Stein goal . . .

41

How Celtic won the Cup

by MAX MARQUIS
(The Sunday Times)

Celtic . . . 4 (3)   Rangers . . . 0 (0)

THE 1969 Scottish Cup Final was bound to be a record-breaking one, whoever the winners, for both Celtic and Rangers had won the trophy nineteen times previously: the winners now would be setting a new club record of twenty Final victories. It was also the "rubber" match between the two teams in Finals. In their previous seven meetings, each club had won the Cup three times, with the trophy being withheld in 1909 after two drawn games.

In fact, despite their recent dismal form, Rangers started fractional favourites. True, they were without their principal striker, Colin Stein, Scotland's first £100,000 player, who was suspended. But Celtic's Jimmy Johnstone was out, too, also suspended—and at the last moment came the shattering news for Celtic supporters that John Hughes, their other world-class winger, was unfit.

Some observers considered that Celtic might even play for a draw, planning to win a replay the following Wednesday, when Hughes was expected to be fit. (In fact, Hughes withdrew from the Scotland squad for the next week's international with Wales at Wrexham.)

The end of a perfect day. It's champagne for happy Tommy Gemmell and another Cup victory for Celtic

THE GOALS: McNEILL HEADS No. 1

*It's a gift. A corner-kick floats into the Rangers'
goalmouth and unmarked McNeill has all the time in
the world to head an easy goal*

Whatever Celtic may have planned before the kick-off,
less than two minutes after it they were a goal up and all set
to contain Rangers, leaving only Chalmers and Lennox
upfield in attack.

When Lennox took a corner on the left, McNeill trotted
up into the Rangers' penalty area. Ferguson, replacing Stein,
went with him. But when the ball came over, McNeill was
completely unmarked. And when he headed the ball
accurately, but with only moderate force, towards the
left-hand post, there was no Rangers defender there covering
it. It was a gift goal.

Celtic immediately surrendered the midfield to Rangers,
but the Ibrox men could not pull their game together. Even
though Celtic had their own moments of uncertainty in
defence in the early stages, Rangers had only two real shots

LENNOX MAKES IT TWO

Another error by Rangers, a poorly judged back pass, and Lennox runs through a bewildered defence to score Celtic's second goal just before half-time

at goal in the entire first half. Fallon saved well from Persson after Mathieson had overlapped down the left, and Greig almost surprised Fallon from Smith's pass. The ball bounced out of the goalkeeper's arms, but Ferguson, rushing in, was just out of reach.

It was a bitter, bruising first half with some terrifying tackles and with players squaring up to each other. Brogan had his name taken for tripping Henderson, but there were many worse fouls; and half a dozen men deserved booking.

In the final couple of minutes before half-time Rangers made two disastrous errors. Celtic pounced, and destroyed them.

Persson's poor back pass towards Mathieson let in Lennox to run on 25 yards and score a goal of monumental calmness in the midst of turmoil. Then Greig bumbled Martin's kick from the six-yard line, and the 20-year-old Connelly took the ball from him, ran on, drew Martin from his goal, waltzed round him and prodded the ball into the empty net.

When Rangers dragged off at half-time they must have known that nothing less than an earthquake could save them.

45

CONNELLY STABS HOME No. 3

Nothing goes well for Rangers. This time it's a bumbled goal-kick, and Connelly is on the spot to give Celtic a three-goal lead at the interval

CHALMERS SNATCHES No. 4

This is a cheeky goal which Celtic's inside-right Chalmers snatches with a fine shot which bends into the net between post and goalkeeper Martin

There was less bite in the second half, but still far too much unpleasantness. The result now was certain: Rangers were playing to save some shreds of individual honour—as a team they had long since been sunk without trace because of their own mistakes. And they were still making them: Lennox headed on to the angle of the bar and a post after a mix-up between McKinnon and Martin.

Brogan limped off reluctantly and was replaced by Clark in the 57th minute, but his defensive abilities were not really needed.

Less than a quarter of an hour before the official end Chalmers broke free, darted down the left wing, then bore in before beating Martin with an unexpected, cheeky right-footed bender of a shot inside the near post.

At this, thousands of Rangers fans poured down the terracing, across the track and behind Martin's goal to the exits, out of sight of their team's misery. They missed one of Rangers' few real goal threats: a shot from Johnston—but the consolation of even one goal was denied them by Fallon's fine leaping save.

Celtic's performance—particularly the darting threats of Chalmers and Lennox—without their two great wingers was impressive enough. What it would be like with them is enough to make the top English clubs think—and think hard.

The teams:

Celtic—Fallon; Craig, Gemmell; Murdoch, McNeill, Brogan; Connelly, Chalmers, Wallace, Lennox, Auld. Sub: Clark.

Rangers—Martin; Johansen, Mathieson; Greig, McKinnon, D. Smith; Henderson, Penman, Ferguson, Johnston, Persson. Sub: Jardine.

JUBILATION

The Cup Final is barely two minutes old and McNeill has given Celtic a surprise lead. Small wonder he leaps for joy

Above: *No, it's not a friendly game of leap-frog in the Celtic goal-mouth: full-back Craig is after the ball, determined that Johnston shall not shoot*

Perfect style, balance and poise from Celtic's inside-right Chalmers as he shoots for goal. Rangers man Greig seems full of admiration

50

Above: *Now the pressure is on Celtic but here Craig appears to be winning this duel with Persson*

Little style about this mix-up which involves Lennox (Celtic) and Greig (Rangers). A high ball has taken them both by surprise

51

SPLIT SECOND TIMING: *Celtic goalkeeper Fallon (that's him in the yellow jersey) shows his form as he neatly catches a high centre despite being jostled by Johnston (Rangers) and Gemmell, one of his own men*

TIME FOR CONTEMPLATION: *Spare a thought for Rangers' goalkeeper Martin. He's had an unhappy afternoon. Four goals have gone past him. Who'd be a goalkeeper?*

. . . and now, Celtic's League Cup Victory

Pressure is applied on the Hibernian goal and goalkeeper Allan punches the ball clear from the airborne McNeill. Lennox stands by, waiting for his chance

Above: *A fine piece of work by Bertie Auld as he scores Celtic's second goal despite the close attention of defenders (left to right) Stanton, Madsen and Davis*

Below: *A Celtic victory is well on its way. Goalkeeper Allan is beaten all ends up as Lennox scores his side's third goal*

VICTORY IS THE TOAST

Celtic celebrate their League Cup success in the dressing-room at Hampden. But where's the champagne?

Jock Stein
makes them
feel so superior

by STEWART BROWN

(Edinburgh Evening News)

WHEN JOCK STEIN stepped into the managerial business in March 1960 he might have been regarded as an enthusiastic and courageous newcomer in taking over a Dunfermline team which seemed bound for the Second Division. But the burly, bluff man who was to become one of the greatest football bosses of all time gave warning of formidable feats to come by transforming the small-time Fifers into an unbeatable outfit.

Under Stein's gifted leadership Dunfermline won their

DUKLA ARE DEFEATED: *Under the bright, cold floodlights Willie Wallace (right) heads a Celtic goal against the highly respected Czech team*

last six matches, during which they ended a Kilmarnock run of eighteen matches without defeat.

There were some who regarded Dunfermline's escape as a fluke, but Stein made the doubtful ones sit up sharply when the Fifers lifted the Scottish Cup in the following season and earned the right to play in Europe. In the four fruitful years he spent at East End Park, Dunfermline became a highly respected team—the club's ultra-modern stand is a per-

Dukla are beaten on their own ground and in front of their own fans. Gemmell and Johnstone greet the victory in swapped Czech shirts

manent monument to his effort on their behalf. Stein is a man with a tremendous flair for tactics and psychology. Charlie Dickson, the Dunfermline centre-forward of the early sixties recalls: "Even when he first joined us his idea was to make us feel superior to the opposition. The message got through to the players. We felt capable of beating any team."

So in 1964 Stein accepted an offer to manage Hibs, a great

post-war team then in the doldrums. Again his presence had an amazing effect on the staff. With a subtle change here and there, they won the Summer Cup, became title challengers and reached the semi-final of the Scottish Cup.

But ten success-packed months after setting Easter Road alight, Stein dropped a bombshell by quitting to go to Celtic . . . the job he had wanted ever since an ankle injury put a premature stop to his playing career in 1957, when he became Celtic coach.

Instead of maybe steering Hibs to a major honour, it was Celtic who won the Scottish Cup under his command, the first of numerous trophies to land at Paradise.

His uncanny knack of moulding victorious teams prompted the S.F.A. to choose him as Scotland team boss in succession to Ian McColl. Stein knew the twin-task would be a burden

but he agreed to take charge of the national squad while they were involved in the World Cup. His term of office lasted from May to December, the month in which a hastily recast and makeshift team bowed out of the tournament in Naples where the volatile fans cheered a 3–0 win for Italy.

His boundless energy was concentrated on making Celtic greater than ever and he carried them into the European Cup by lifting the championship in 1966. It was Celtic's first flag for twelve years. (Stein was a member of the team which pulled off the Cup and League double in 1953–54 and which also won the Coronation Cup under his captaincy.)

And, at the first time of asking, Celtic became kings of Europe. What a season it was for Stein and his invincibles! They made a clean sweep of every competition they played in, winning the Championship, League Cup, Scottish Cup and

INTER MILAN: ONE THAT DIDN'T GO IN

This is the European Cup Final, Celtic's finest hour and one of outstanding achievement. The Scots are after goals but —believe it or not—this shot from Chalmers was saved on the line by goalkeeper Sarti

. . . AND ONE THAT DID

This time Sarti fails to reach a fierce shot from Gemmell and it's a goal which puts the Scots back on level terms with the Italians

HE'S A SCOTTISH HERO

The European Cup has been won after a hard match
—and shirtless Billy McNeill, Celtic's captain, runs
the gauntlet of fans on the Inter Milan ground

Glasgow Cup before their finest 90 minutes in Lisbon's National Stadium.

They played 62 competitive games; won 51 and lost 3; and the team's dynamic attacking football produced 196 goals for the loss of 48.

The European campaign was carefully planned from one stage to the next. Zurich and Nantes were disposed of comfortably and then came their only defeat, a 1–0 setback against Vojvodina, a strong, physical and talented team from Yugoslavia. Even in front of their own singing thousands, Celtic found it hard and it took a late headed goal by Billy McNeill to earn the semi-final place.

It was in Prague against Dukla, who trailed 3–1, that Stein

HERO WORSHIP AT PARKHEAD

Celtic are back in Glasgow with the much-coveted European Cup in their possession. It's a great moment in the history of Scottish football—and 60,000 roaring Celtic fans acknowledge the tremendous achievement. Will there ever be another homecoming like this?

showed Celtic in a new light. He gave his goal-conscious team a new task: to prevent the Czechs from scoring. The goal-less draw illustrated how well they had carried out his battle orders.

But there was no negative play against Inter Milan, the defensive masters, in the final. The loss of an early penalty by Mazzola did not prevent Celtic from producing the best football in a European trophy match since Real Madrid's Hampden triumph over Eintracht in 1960. Goals by full-back

JOCK STEIN: *He has taken his team to dizzy heights—and now the European Cup is in his grasp. With him here is right-back Bobby Murdoch*

Tommy Gemmell and centre-forward Steve Chalmers gave Stein his proudest moments. Celtic won the trophy with a team that cost a little over £30,000; a remarkable effort by a man who has never fancied handing out huge cheques.

He paid Hearts £29,000 for striker Willie Wallace, who repaid the fee with two goals against Dukla. And a small sum changed hands when Stein took veteran goalkeeper Ronnie Simpson from Hibs to Celtic Park. The rest of the players had been signed from the minor grades by Stein or other Celtic backroom boys.

No world-class side ever cost so little to put together. And instead of the foreign newspapers carrying stories about the deeds of Herrera, Munoz or Guttmann, it was Stein who captured the headlines. Nobody, in fact, is more adept at projecting the image of Celtic. Scottish football hasn't known a press relations officer of Jock's standing, for he is peerless in the art of releasing news.

Having driven Celtic to the grand slam it was felt that he might seek a new challenge elsewhere; his name was frequently mentioned as a likely successor to Sir Matt Busby with Manchester United. But he put a lot of minds at rest this year by stating that he would remain at Parkhead to the end of his managerial days at the age of 55.

Jock reckons that is long enough to bear the strain of modern management. Born in Burnbank, an ex-miner, and a former centre-half of Albion Rovers, Llanelly and Celtic, he is 46, which gives him another nine years of globe-trotting and honours with Celtic. He has a grown-up daughter and a son nearing the end of his schooldays. Although he enjoys an afternoon at the races and a relaxing game of golf, he scarcely ever unwinds and simply loves to talk football. His whole life revolves around the game. He is a father-figure to his players from the most important member of the side to the newest ground-staff boy.

Every player who has served him idolises the "big man" because the welfare of his boys is the thing that matters most to him. He is edgy during matches and has landed in trouble with authority for sniping at referees. Stein admits that his feelings towards match officials at the conclusion of a game have always altered by the time he writes his report on a Monday morning.

The Celtic ground is known as Paradise. Stein has made that name ring true.

1879
*William Dunlop, Club president and
a footballer of note*

1969
*John Lawrence, Club chairman,
millionaire — and proud of Rangers*

68

Glasgow Rangers

by WILLIE ALLISON

*(Ex-Sunday Mail columnist, now Director of
Publicity, Glasgow Rangers)*

GLASGOW RANGERS! You love them with a fanatical
pride and devotion—or you loathe them with an insensate
hate. There is no middle emotion for a Scottish football fan.

Glasgow Rangers—there is no greater romance in sport
than the birth of this mighty club. It grew from its humble
inception in 1873 to become a world power. Those laughing,
lusty lads of 1873 pulled their rowing-boats ashore on the
upper reaches of the Clyde, became absorbed in the new sport
—soccer—and decided to start a club on their own.

The thrill and non-stop action of soccer excited them and as
their enthusiasm for rowing dwindled and vanished, the
challenge of football brought them new adventures. Those
sportsmen from the river never realised that their decision
would have such extraordinary consequences. For over the
years Rangers have lived to set up records on the domestic
front which none has surpassed.

Although they have not matched the feat of their arch-
rivals, Celtic, in winning the European Cup, they are record
holders of the League Championship trophy with 34 wins:
they have 19 Scottish Cup-final victories; they have won the
Scottish League Cup a record 10 times (the Southern League
Cup and the Scottish League Cup are the same tournament
with different trophies). The Glasgow Charity they have won
32 times, and the Glasgow Cup 35 times. The Victory Cup,
which they hold in perpetuity, and which was put up in place

SCOTTISH CUP FINAL TEAM, 1876—1877.

Back Row—George Gillespie, William M'Neil, Tom Vallance, and J. M. Watt.
Middle Row—William Dunlop, David Hill, Peter Campbell, Moses M'Neil, and Sam Ricketts.
Front Row—James A. K. Watson and A. Marshall.

The year is 1877 and it is the first Rangers' team, despite the unfamiliar jerseys, that played in a Scottish Cup final. Opponents were the now disbanded Vale of Leven. Twice the games were drawn, 0—0 and 1—1, at Hamilton Crescent. In the second replay at Hampden Park Rangers lost 3—2

of the Scottish Cup at the end of the last war, also rests in their glittering trophy room.

It is in that room, incidentally, that you will see a portrait of the legendary Bill Struth, who sat for the painting knowing he hadn't many days to live. It was Struth who guided the Rangers to their days of greatness. He created a tradition, as did William Wilton before him, that formed the real starting-point of the club's achievement.

Followed by manager Scot Symon and now by David

FIRST *Rangers* TEAM TO WIN THE SCOTTISH CUP, 1893-1894.

J. Taylor (*Trainer*).
Back Row—H. M'Creadie, J. Steel, N. Smith, D. Haddow, D. Mitchell.
Sitting—A. M'Creadie, D. Boyd, W. Wilton (*Secretary*), J. Drummond, J. MacPherson, J. Barker.
Front Row—R. Marshall, J. Gray.
Scottish Cup.   Glasgow Cup.

Success at last. The year is 1894, and Rangers win the Scottish Cup for the first time. It was a proud season, for they also won the Glasgow Cup. Fashion note: The knee-length shorts are a long way removed from present-day briefs

White, the Struth era was one of grim, no-team-is-our-equal conviction. What Struth might have done in this modern age with its altered techniques and fetish for jet-paced forwards can only be a matter of conjecture, but the records created during his reign bear witness to his remarkable ability to compromise—and demand.

But the past fades. The new boss at Ibrox, and his assistant, ex-Rangers' centre Willie Thornton, fix their sights on Europe.

With Ibrox Stadium built to hold 126,000 (with cover for

LEAGUE RECORD CHAMPIONS, 1898—1899.
Played 18; Won 18; Lost 0; Drawn 0.

Back Row—J. Wilson (*Trainer*), J. Henderson (*President*), N. Smith, D. Crawford, N. Gibson, M. Dickie, J. Stark,
R. G. Neil, J. T. Robertson, J. Drummond, W. Wilton (*Hon. Match Secretary*), A. B. Mackenzie (*Committee*).
Sitting—J. Campbell, J. Graham, J. MacPherson, R. C. Hamilton (*Captain*), F. Speedie, And. Sharp, A. Smith.
Insets—J. Miller, D. Mitchell, J. Wilkie, T. Hyslop.

Who remembers this line-up? These men set up a British record when, in 1898–99, Glasgow Rangers won every match in the League Championship. They scored 79 goals and conceded only 18. The sides which were so convincingly beaten were: Celtic, Hearts, Hibernian, Third Lanark, St. Mirren, St. Bernards, Clyde, Dundee and Partick Thistle

65,000 and tip-up seats for 10,294), Rangers can earn more than £35,000 for almost any home fixture against top European opposition. Football has become big business in Scotland—at any rate for Rangers and Celtic—as it has been for some time now in England and among the fashionable Continental and South American clubs.

Now Rangers can afford to pay £100,000 transfer fees, as they did for Colin Stein from Hibernian. They have come a

72

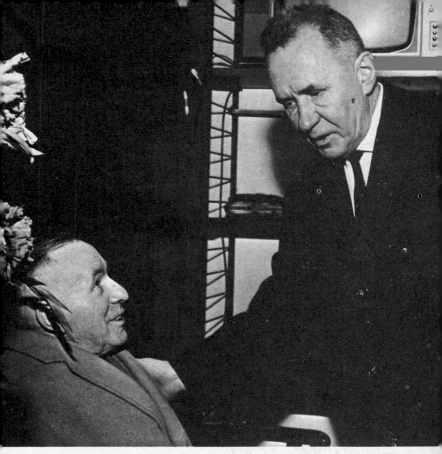

When Russia's President Kosygin visited Scotland it was known he was a keen football fan and he was taken to see a match, Kilmarnock v. Rangers at Rugby Park. He presented the Rangers with a crystal football and was introduced (above) to club director Alan Morton, one of the finest left-wingers Rangers and Scotland have ever produced

long way from the day in the 1880s when the Rangers' chairman lent the club £30 to save it from bankruptcy.

But away from this remarkable story of progress there is a primitive attitude which stains the names of Scotland's two great clubs. While the great majority of both Rangers and Celtic fans are law-abiding citizens, there is a minority who

73

under the name of religion, defile the reputations of both clubs. Fines, gaol sentences and severe warnings have been imposed but these rowdies still disturb the peace in our crowds.

The police have worked closely with the clubs, and plain-clothed officers haul the hooligans out of the crowds. Rangers, in their turn, keep a record of the names and addresses of all those charged in court for offences at Ibrox and send these undesirables letters telling them that they will never again be admitted to a Rangers' home match. The club has also decided to appoint stewards who will point out to the police anyone who tries to enter the ground under the influence of drink or who tries to take drink into the stadium.

Against the spasmodic outbreaks of violence can be set the pageantry of football fashioned through the years by the great ones who wore Ibrox colours. Let it not be forgotten that since 1873 Rangers have provided Scotland with 1,192 international players, a world record. Heroes like the peerless Alan Morton, the Wee Blue Devil, who gained his nickname by tormenting many an English defence; Jimmy Gordon, who played both for Rangers and Scotland in almost every position on the field; the incomparable Neilly Gibson, lion-hearted Davie Meiklejohn, George Brown (now, like Alan Morton, a director of the club), George Young, Willie Thornton, that deadly header of the ball, and now Colin Stein.

All these and so many more—not forgetting Lil' Arthur Dixon, the centre-half from Oldham, who on his deathbed murmured, "I'm an Englishman, but my happiest days were with Rangers. It is my wish that my ashes be scattered on the Ibrox field which I loved so well." His wish was granted.

Past glories, however, can often obscure the effort and brilliance of the present generation of players. Today the Rangers' side has men who have inherited the tradition of the past and have shown themselves worthy of it. Captain John Greig, discovered as a raw lad during Rangers' unbeaten tour of Russia, has skippered Scotland three times against England and has been made "Player of the Year" by the world-wide legion of Rangers supporters.

There's the dashing Dane, Kaj Johansen, who scored

*A Rangers partnership — Willie Mathieson and John Greig —
stop Willie Hamilton (Hearts) from going through with the ball*

the wonder goal that gave Rangers the Scottish Cup in their
epic replay final against Celtic in 1966 at Hampden; there's
Ronnie McKinnon, who is rated the toughest but safest
tackler in Europe. And with an attack that includes Willie
Henderson, Andy Penman, Colin Stein, Billy Johnston and
Orjan Persson, Rangers are the envy of Scotland.

It is no wonder, then, that the shout, "Follow, follow, we
will follow Rangers" has now reached a fortissimo note. The
Rangers of today, possessed of an explosive splendour and
pugnacity, must fully recapture the reputation that was theirs
before the three years of bitter frustration and failure to win
a major trophy.

Believe me, a new era is opening at Ibrox.

75

Johansen is an Ibrox favourite. He's a difficult man to pass —
as Gilshan, of St. Mirren, knows only too well

Right: Aberdeen's defence is in a state of panic and the
man who has got it that way is Rangers' Ron McKinnon.
The Aberdeen full-back (No. 2) is Jimmy Smith

This is Willie Johnston, a modern Ranger who rarely lets a chance slip by. He always has his sights trained on the opposition's goal

79

Andy Penman has poise and a remarkable ability which places him among the Rangers' giants

Willie Henderson is a Rangers wizard, a match-winner for his club and for Scotland. **Above left** *he dribbles past Dundee United's Alex Reid.* **Below:** *The little winger tries to jump over John Clark's leg in a tackle during a match against Celtic*

Colin Stein is Rangers' player of the moment. He cost them £100,000 but it's agreed he'll repay the Ibrox club in full and with a big dividend. The pictures on these two pages display his determination and courage

Ferguson boots the ball over the bar, watched by team-mates Stein and Johnston

Right: *This is true Rangers style and the man putting it on view is Orjan Persson*

The last man in defence—goalkeeper Martin. The ball is safely in his hands before Wallace, of Celtic, moves in to challenge

Right: A new boy on the Ibrox scene, goalkeeper Gerhard Neef, who shows his outstanding ability during his début against Morton. A Rangers star in the making?

Why footballers won't stay in the north

by NORMAN MACDONALD

(Sports Editor, Aberdeen Journals Ltd.)

SCOTLAND'S three most northerly senior clubs have one problem in common—how to retain their personality players in face of lucrative offers from the wealthier English League clubs.

There have been occasions when Scottish clubs have been reluctant to do business. Aberdeen are a case in point. At the start of last season the Pittodrie officials turned down tempting offers from Celtic and Liverpool for the transfer of inside-forward Jimmy Smith. But in the final analysis money talks, and it is no secret that Scottish clubs, with the possible exception of Rangers and Celtic, are happy to accept English cash in order to survive financially.

How, for instance, could Aberdeen refuse the £100,000 offered by Sheffield Wednesday for teenage wing-half Tommy Craig? But most of this cash will be used to improve the Pittodrie playing staff.

Aberdeen's need to transfer star players is less urgent than that of their rivals. How Dundee must envy the Granite City, outpost of senior football in Scotland! The two cities have populations of comparable size, but Aberdeen, with only one club, have virtually a monopoly over a wide area. Dundee, on the other hand, with two First Division clubs, is a city of divided loyalties. While Aberdeen is free from

A young Scot who has moved south from Aberdeen to cross the Border for a new career with Sheffield Wednesday. What does the future hold for Tommy Craig?

competition, the Dundee clubs have to contend with six First and Second Division clubs within a 30 miles radius. The Dundee clubs can truly be described as near neighbours, for you could toss a stone from Dens Park to Tannadice Park.

Aberdeen can put forward a strong claim to be the best supported club in Scotland outside Glasgow and there is clear proof that a successful Dons team, challenging for honours, unlike their rivals, could survive on the money paid at the turnstiles.

Confronted with declining attendances, Dundee and Dundee United must come up with a scheme to create a resurgence of interest in the city in the new season. Dundee United manager Jerry Kerr, who has the distinction of being the longest-serving manager in Scotland, must wonder what he has to do to attract economic crowds to Tannadice.

The signing of Kenny Cameron from Kilmarnock added the missing punch in attack; so successful have the United been in the past season that they were rarely missing from the leading six clubs in the First Division table. Yet their average gate must be in the region of 6,000 to 7,000. Fortunately, the

Andy Penman, the man in the dark shirt, was a star with Dundee before he joined Rangers

90

Right: *Alan Gilzean when he was a goal-scoring favourite at Dens Park before he left to take up residence with fashionable Tottenham Hotspur*

club operates one of the most successful development schemes in Scotland. But it is surely a sad commentary on the Dundee soccer public that they can show no more than a lukewarm interest in a successful team.

And manager Jerry Kerr certainly can't be accused of lack of enterprise. Unable to meet the market price demanded for experienced players in this country, Dundee United were one of the first clubs to realise the potentialities of the Scandinavian countries as a source of ready-made talent. In the season 1964 65 Kerr signed Finn Dossing and Mogens Berg from Denmark and Orjan Persson and Lennart Wing from Sweden, and in the following season Finn Seeman joined the Tannadice staff from Norway. All five players made quite an impact on Scottish football.

Dundee are no more successful than their neighbours in their efforts to woo the Dundee public and, without the assistance of a development scheme, they have their financial worries. The situation must have been eased, temporarily at any rate, last March, when they transferred inside-forward George McLean to Dunfermline for a £22,000 fee.

It is difficult to find a valid explanation for the decline in attendances at Dens Park—it is reckoned that gates are in the region of half what they were five years ago. Dundee have never touched the heights of brilliance they achieved in 1962, when they won the Scottish League championship; interest seems to have waned with the departure of such stars as Andy Penman, Alan Cousin, Alan Gilzean and Hugh Robertson.

Now former Scotland team manager John Prentice has been given the job of putting a new gloss on the Dens Park image. Mr. Prentice joined Dundee from Falkirk in September 1968 after holding managerial posts at Arbroath and Clyde. He ran the Shawfield club successfully with a limited pool of players. In an effort to trim costs at Dundee he may well consider a similar operation at Dens Park.

After spending £50,000 for the transfers of Jim Forrest from Preston North End and Tommy Rae from Partick Thistle, Aberdeen were expected to come forward with a strong challenge for honours last season. Aberdeen's manager Eddie Turnbull was as mystified as the north-east

*Dundee's coffers bene-
fitted when George
McLean was transfer-
red to Dunfermline for
a £22,000 fee*

public by the team's incredibly inconsistent form.

Despite the fact that instead of emerging as challengers to Rangers and Celtic the Dons were involved in the struggle to avoid relegation in the closing weeks of the season, the crowds continued to turn out at Pittodrie and home gates almost always topped the five-figure mark.

Recent ground improvements have made Pittodrie one of the neatest and most compact enclosures in Scotland. The stadium is capable of holding over 50,000 with seating accommodation for over 5,000 and covered shelter for 25,000. Now manager Turnbull's aim for the new season is to field a team to match the ground amenities.

Dundee, Dundee United and Aberdeen have all made appearances in European competitions and the Dens Park club has the distinction of having played in all three major tournaments. Dundee reached the semi-final stages of the European Cup and the Inter-cities Fairs Cup. In the European Cup they were beaten by Milan, who went on to win the trophy. They went under to Leeds United in the semi-final of the Fairs Cup in season 1967–68.

A challenge for the Scottish League championship flag is overdue from the far North clubs. Will it come from Dens Park, Tannadice or Pittodrie?

Who can challenge the Old Firm?

by DOUGLAS RITCHIE
(The Sun)

RANGERS AND CELTIC stand supreme. They monopolise the honours, the headlines and the adherence of a very large proportion of Scotland's fans. They are the giants at home— the championship is normally a two-club race—and between them they carry Scotland's football torch in Europe.

But where is the David who can topple these twin Goliaths? The challenge is now a part of Scottish football life.

Consider the advantages which the Old Firm enjoy: for a start, there's all that gold in the coffers at Ibrox Stadium and Celtic Park. For instance, Rangers have spent almost half a million pounds in recent seasons trying to buy their way out of the stranglehold Celtic have put on Scottish football in the Jock Stein era of glory. Celtic have been more conservative—but they have bought, too.

Every time the Old Firm moves into the transfer market the challenge is automatically weakened. On the sheer economics of the game other clubs find it almost impossible to stave off these raids on their talents. They do not get enough revenue through the turnstiles to make them financially independent. They have to sell, if not to Rangers or Celtic then to one of the South-of-the-Border giants.

Rangers and Celtic can keep their players: they have the means to pay the highest wages and the biggest bonuses. And

*A moment George Farm will remember for a long time.
His team, Dunfermline, have just knocked Celtic out
of the Cup—and in 1968 that was no mean feat*

how can part-time clubs such as Airdrie or St. Mirren deny players the chance to pick up the big pay packets?

How then can clubs possibly shoot for what would seem to be the impossible? Some have made the effort with flickering success, including Hearts, Aberdeen, Dundee United and Hibs, but the effort has never been sustained.

Yet there *are* two clubs making threatening noises right now—Dunfermline Athletic and Kilmarnock. Both have young driving managers—George Farm with Dunfermline and Walter McCrae with Kilmarnock: men with a mission—to smash the Old Firm supremacy.

Dunfermline won the Scottish Cup at Hampden last year; Kilmarnock, the record losers in championship and cup, broke through for a title win. Dunfermline have not escaped the Old Firm transfer net—they have lost Alex Smith and Alex Ferguson to Rangers, Tom Callaghan to Celtic. But they have used the money to buy replacements at their own

Now it's Rangers who come under pressure from the
Dunfermline attack. Goalkeeper Martin is lucky to flick the
ball away from the head of Johnston

Left: Celtic star, Johnstone, is hard pressed by two of
Dunfermline's energetic men, Lunn and Barry. The Old Firm
keeps a sharp watch on men such as these

transfer level. Kilmarnock have bought within their means, too.

These two clubs have faced the economics of Scottish football—and that could be the first breakthrough towards catching the Old Firm. Dunfermline have given their manager a brand-new five years' contract. They want to maintain continuity at the top.

A moment of fierce Cup action between Hearts and Dunfermline. Centre-forward Gardner gets a sight of goal and the ball is in the net. The Fifers are on the way to Cup glory

These, then, are the new pretenders. Can they bring down the giants? At any rate, it's obvious that they really mean to have a good try.

When the Old Firm didn't get a look-in. . . . This time it's Dunfermline and manager George Farm who celebrate a Cup victory at Hampden and drink the traditional champagne

A threat to Dunfermline—this time from Partick Thistle. In this goalmouth tussle Roy Barry (Dunfermline) gets the high ball away from Bone and McLindon

Everything clicks into place for Dunfermline. It's a perfect header and a picture-book goal for Fraser in a match against St. Mirren

103

Can Kilmarnock upset the balance of power? The task is formidable. . . . **Below**: *Kilmarnock's McIlroy takes the ball past right-back Whyte, of Aberdeen, at Rugby Park.* **Right, above**: *An anxious moment against Celtic as left-back Dickson watches a shot from Johnstone whistle goalwards.* **Right, below**: *In a tough match against Rangers there's nothing defenders King, McLaughlan and McGrory can do to stop a Willie Henderson pile-driver*

Dunfermline goalkeeper Martin makes his job look easy as he clears a Kilmarnock attack. Centre-half Barry stands guard as Martin teases little Tommy McLean

Waiting for their chance, Kilmarnock players McIlroy and Morrison are beaten to the ball by Aberdeen goalkeeper McGarr

Goalkeeping is in my blood!

by JIM CRUICKSHANK
(Heart of Midlothian)

THERE ARE TIMES when it isn't much fun being a goal-keeper. Like the day I lost 11 goals, or the game I can't remember because a kick on the ear gave me concussion. But I wouldn't change my position for any other in the game.

Fortunately, I have had a fairly injury-free career; I hope my luck holds for a few more years. That bout of concussion is the worst thing that ever happened to me. Hearts were playing Dunfermline in a Summer Cup match in May 1964, and I dived at the feet of Alex Ferguson and Bert Paton as they charged in on a loose ball. One of them caught me behind the ear with his boot but, after a spot of treatment, I managed to carry on. I went in at half-time feeling a bit dazed but I had no thought of staying in the dressing-room.

It wasn't until the second half that the blow really took effect. Hearts had a tour of America about to start and, in my dazed condition, I began to ask my colleagues if we had been to the States. . . . I wanted to know if this was the start of a new season. My babblings didn't make any sense to them at all. At the finish, two players had to help me into the showers in case I collapsed but, at least, they didn't take me to hospital—I was driven home to rest.

There was a happy ending to the episode: we beat Dunfermline 2–1.

The goalkeeper is a team's last line of defence, sometimes an unenviable position. But Jim Cruick-shank wouldn't change

The crowd roars its appreciation when a goalkeeper saves a "certain" goal . . . and here, Jim Cruickshank is doing just that against Rangers at Ibrox

As a Queen's Park teenager I spent a fortnight in hospital with knee trouble that lasted for four months and which resulted in a cartilage operation. Strangely enough, it was not an injury that caused the trouble—the damage was done by kicking a dead ball.

Then in last year's Scottish Cup final—against Dunfermline again—I took a sore knock on the ankle. It wasn't something that could be blamed on an opponent: the man responsible was my own centre-half, Arthur Thomson, who accidentally crippled me. Soon after the final—which we lost

But it's moans and groans when the ball goes into the net—especially when it happens in a local derby. Cruickshank knows what some of the Hearts' fans are saying as he fails to stop this hot shot from Jimmy O'Rourke, of Hibs

—Hearts went on a tour in Ireland, but that ankle injury prevented me from playing in more than one game. It was as well for me that the season was over!

Naturally, I've had my share of scrapes and bruises. Last season I injured a finger on my left hand in a game against Clyde and spent an agonising afternoon. My left hand was useless—and Hearts lost 3–2.

Only my pride was hurt, though, on the day that I lost double figures in my home town. It was soon after I joined Hearts and we were playing Rangers in a reserve match at Ibrox. It was a miserable, foggy day and nobody imagined that the game would go on. Looking back, I wish the fog had been worse—even denser—it would have spared me the embarrassment of watching the ghostly figure of Jim Forrest slamming goal after goal into my net. Jim, now with Aberdeen, could do nothing wrong: he scored seven goals that disastrous afternoon. I could do nothing right, as the 11–1 score so plainly reflected.

111

Another black day for me and for Hearts was when Dundee crushed us 7–1 at Tynecastle. It was bad enough at the time, but a lot worse when Kilmarnock lifted the championship on goal average on the last day of the season by beating us at home.

I reckon that Rangers pose the biggest problems for me these days and, of course, there is Tommy McLean, the Kilmarnock and Scotland winger. He crosses a great ball. Little McLean is no friend of goalkeepers in the course of a game. He tantalises you with a perfectly flighted centre, and just as you think it is sailing into your hands, the ball veers dangerously away to a waiting head. In my ten years with Hearts—I'm their longest-serving player—I haven't met any other forward with the same flair for troubling me with cross balls.

At 27, I must have several years left in the game, especially if you think in terms of Ronnie Simpson, who isn't far off the 40 mark. Not that we can all expect to go on as long as Ronnie.

I regret not having represented my country more often, but it's my own fault to an extent. I was groomed in the Scotland amateur team during my Queen's Park days and played for the Under-23 team while I was still a schoolboy. My only big cap was against West Germany in 1964—just a few days after my concussion. The match was in Hanover and I was quite satisfied with my own game; we drew 2–2 with our powerful hosts. The great Uwe Seeler beat me twice and Alan Gilzean got a couple of goals for us. The inside forwards in our team were Denis Law and the late John White, a fine partnership.

I was picked for the Scotland tour in the summer of 1967 and we visited such places as Hong Kong, Israel, Australia, Canada and New Zealand in an unbeaten trip against opposition that didn't extend us. I shared the goalkeeping duties with Harry Thomson, of Burnley, but my heart wasn't in the game on the tour for I had become unsettled with Hearts. My intention was to move to another club and, as a result of being discontented, my form suffered. I know that I didn't help my future prospects in that series of games abroad.

One remaining ambition of mine is to play against England at Wembley. I haven't given up hope even if the chance only comes along every two years.

Last season I had the honour of captaining Hearts for most of the season after skipper Jim Townsend had broken his ankle at Falkirk.

Some players find that their game is affected by the leadership. It does not bother me. I enjoyed the additional responsibility; being captain spurred me to play better. I must admit, however, that the ideal position for a captain is wing-half. A disadvantage of being goalie-captain is that your colleagues don't always hear when you shout some instruction from the goalmouth.

Continental referees are a big problem

by BOB SHANKLY

(Hibernian's manager)

THERE IS NO GREATER stimulus for a team's supporters than to be involved in one of the three European tournaments. Even if your club has no chance of the championship, a good run to the late stages of a competition can keep interest at fever pitch. I know how much it has meant to Hibs in the past couple of seasons and to other clubs out of the trophy hunt.

Playing all over the Continent brings many strains. Over a six-year period I have had a stake in 25 matches with Dundee and Hibs covering the European Cup, the Cup Winners Cup and the Fairs Cup. I have been in seven countries, many of them more than once, and found the same old problems cropping up every time.

The main complaint of all managers is the refereeing. Despite attempts through the years to find universal interpretations we still find an official from Yugoslavia, for instance, reacting differently from one from Spain.

When I stepped on to the European merry-go-round in 1962 Dundee were the League winners—and I was thrown into the European Cup struggle. I'll never forget it. . . .

We were drawn against Cologne and the Germans sent over a "spy" who stayed in Dundee for a month and reported on our matches. He sent back stories of an out-of-form team. Cologne, who had just won the new Super League, reckoned

On the Continent "the main complaint of all managers is the refereeing", says Bob Shankly

they were as good as through to round two. But Dundee had a severe shock in store for them. On a night when absolutely everything went right for us, the Germans were trounced 8–1. The Cologne goalkeeper was taken off at one point supposed to be badly hurt. Actually, he had a cut lip!

The return game looked a formality, but the Germans were thirsting for revenge. They hit us with everything. They laid out goalkeeper Bert Slater; before I could run to him, he had been whipped on to a stretcher and was heading for the local hospital. But we stopped that caper and Slater returned to the field, first at outside-right and later in his own position. However, our seven-goal lead was dwindling. When Cologne were 4–0 up they were awarded a penalty. With almost half

115

an hour to go, another goal would have been disastrous for us. But they missed the penalty and their challenge died.

My players were all aching when they reached the dressing-room; they agreed on the spot to shun the official banquet after the game. They didn't want to feel hypocrites.

The lesson was driven home to me then for the need to be cautious defensively on foreign territory. I also realised that no lead is big enough to justify over-confidence.

Such ties were an education to me; I picked up more tips in those 180 minutes against Cologne than I did in the re-maining six games we played in the European Cup.

You try to catch out an aggressive home team with swift counter-attacks when you are abroad; we did so in the third round against Anderlecht in Belgium. Anderlecht came out to strike quickly and found themselves two down in seven minutes. And the lead, achieved with two forwards up, was increased to 4–1.

My first experience of an awkward referee came in Milan where the Spaniard in charge penalised us throughout the 90 minutes for every triviality he could find. We lost offside goals and had ridiculous free kicks awarded against us. The Italians finished 5–1 ahead. Dundee had gone to the semi-final but the San Siro Stadium was their end of the road.

Two years later we moved into the Cup Winners Cup as runners-up to Rangers. Our stay was short and not so sweet for, after drawing at home with Saragossa, a soft penalty put us out in Spain—just another refereeing break.

I moved to Hibs and they won a place in the Fairs Cup in 1965–66, drawing Valencia in the first round. So it was back to Spain for me. The teams were level on aggregate after the two games and officials of both clubs met in the referee's changing room. The referee was Gottfried Dienst, later to handle the World Cup final at Wembley.

He spun a coin that bounced off a table and rolled under-neath a chair at the wall. People were scrambling about on their knees to see which team had won ground advantage in the decider. Valencia were lucky—and we lost the play-off 3–0. But what a way to go out!

On to Portugal in 1967, and amazing scenes in Porto when we were awarded a penalty inside five minutes. The home players threatened the Spanish referee, pushed him around and broke every rule in the book. Nobody was sent off at this stage, though the game was held up for more than five minutes.

Joe Davis scored with the kick to give us an overall 4–0 lead. That was it, we thought—but we didn't bargain for the sudden swing in the referee's attitude. Porto rapped on three goals and my disillusioned team was on the ropes, gasping for the final whistle that came just in time.

Again our advantage was substantial, yet it was almost not enough.

Our next tie was one for the scrapbook. Naples beat Hibs 4–1 at home and the fiery fans with the bad reputation graciously cheered us out of the stadium. Maybe that was because of the three-goal lead. Our defence had slipped up and the forwards, though able to make countless chances, had finished deplorably.

People in Edinburgh thought I was daft when I claimed that Hibs could qualify. Naples were so confident that they left their star scorer Altafini at home and spent a day in London on their way to Scotland. But we qualified as I had forecast—and what a night that was for the Easter Road crowd! Right-back Bobby Duncan scored the goal that inspired the team to win 5–0.

Hibs were knocked out by Leeds United on a 2–1 aggregate and Don Revie told me at the end of the season that we had been tougher opponents than Rangers and Dundee.

It's an expensive business to charter an aircraft to go abroad, but I wish we had done so last season when we went to Leipzig to play Lokomotive. Bad weather caused us to arrive 24 hours late after long delays in Amsterdam and East Berlin and the subsequent coach journeys were far from comfortable. However, I haven't met any friendlier folk than the East Germans—even in defeat.

Hibs were knocked out by Hamburg—or rather, by the rule which says away goals count double in the event of an aggregate draw. We lost 1–0 in Hamburg and won 2–1 in Edinburgh where we had three goals disallowed. See what I mean about a referee's interpretation? I would prefer a tie to be settled on penalties or corners rather than on the present system. Many football officials agree with me.

Some managers like to spy on foreign opposition, but I don't think it helps much. Sure, I watched Naples against Hanover when we played the winners, but you have to see a team home and away to assess them. And, frankly, there isn't time to do that in a busy Scottish season.

THE DANCE OF DEFENCE

The St. Mirren defenders leap to it — and a shot
from Rangers' Roger Hynd sails over the bar

Best buy of the year–

Crackshot Cameron

WHO WAS the best buy of the year? No doubt about it: stocky Kenny Cameron. It cost Dundee United only £7,500 to buy him from Kilmarnock at the beginning of last season; Manager Jerry Kerr can look upon the signing as one of his most inspired transactions. Cameron had a tremendous season for United. He scored 36 goals in the championship, League Cup and Scottish Cup, to finish as the season's leading goal-scorer in Scottish football.

Cameron signed for Dundee in 1962 and lived in digs in the city. There, he scored 43 goals in the three seasons preceding his transfer to Kilmarnock. But he still lived in Dundee and motored across-country several times each week. Not surprisingly his form took a nose-dive. He began in a blaze of glory and netted eight League Cup goals. Gradually, however, the 6.30 a.m. rise and the many hours of travelling took their toll—he ended the season with only 19 goals. A switch back to Dundee and a transfer to United was the answer.

Cameron is under 5 ft. 8 ins. and weighs $10\frac{1}{2}$ stone so it isn't his physique that makes him a menace in the goal area; it's his quick eye for a chance and his nippiness in moving into the open space.

Dundee United will be back in Europe in the coming season thanks to crackshot Cameron and his highly effective partnership with Ian Mitchell. In their only previous Fairs Cup appearance United knocked out Barcelona, the holders, before falling to Juventus. This time they'll have Scotland's No. 1 goal-getter in their side and that could make a very big difference.

Stewart Brown

Kenny Cameron (9) keeps his eye on the ball, but this time the chance of a goal has gone. The Rangers' goal line is cleared by Ron McKinnon

TWO MEN IN STEP and with a single thought—both Scott (Dundee United), left, and Penman (Rangers) want possession of the ball

THE PERFECT HEADER produced by George McLean
(Dundee). He's closely watched by Thomson and Anderson,
of Hearts

123

NO QUARTER is given or asked in European football. King, of Kilmarnock, knows this only too well as he tussles with an Eintracht player from Frankfurt

THE PILE-DRIVER: Balance, power and perfect coordination by Celtic's Jimmy Johnstone as he rockets the ball towards the goal. Here is the hallmark of a footballing craftsman

124

PROUD MOMENT for Billy Bremner as he leads the Scottish team out on to the pitch at Wembley to face England

ROYAL GREETING for the Scottish players. The Duchess of Kent is introduced to them before the kick-off

The Home International
Championship:

How the Scots went down fighting

by ROGER STANFORD

"IT SHOULD NEVER have been a penalty, and two of the other English goals were offside a mile." That's what Scots international wing-half Pat Crerand said after England had beaten Scotland 4–1 and pipped them for the International Championship at Wembley last May.

In other words, it was as good as a moral victory for

An informal moment for the Scottish team. **Back row** (left to right): Stein, Herriot, Murdoch, Greig, Gilzean, Gray. **Front row**: McNeill, Henderson, Bremner, McCreadie, Gemmell

Scotland. Except for the penalty, I don't think Pat really expected to be taken seriously. But his remark showed the irrepressible nature of the Scots when it comes to battling the "auld enemy".

Pat might just as well have said: "Don't think one victory makes you cock of the walk, England. We'll be back next year." That would have been echoed by thousands of his fellow-countrymen as they made their disappointed way back to the great footballing area between Carlisle and Cape Wrath.

To lose to an England side which even Scottish team manager Bobby Brown described afterwards as "worthy world champions" was no disgrace, even though it meant second place in this first British championship "week" all Scots dearly wanted to win. The great Scots fighting spirit had already manifested itself twice in matches against Wales and Northern Ireland. Perhaps to expect a third soul-stirring rally in eight days of the hardest, most intensive soccer competition to be found anywhere in the world was asking too much of a team which really never had a chance to settle.

But Scotland had plenty of courage and put on some grand displays. For a start, there was the tremendous fight-back at Wrexham against Wales. Billy McNeill's header and Colin Stein's wonder eye-of-the-needle shot through the Welsh defence had the Taffies rattled before they could draw breath. When they pulled the two goals back through Ron Davies and Toshack, many a side seeing such a lead disappearing would have lost heart. Instead, there was Alan Gilzean waiting like a balding hawk to pounce on a Sprake mistake and wee Tommy McLean finally sent the Welsh reeling with a glorious solo effort.

Even in their only home game of the tournament which followed against the Irish, the Scots missed what all the others enjoyed — the full-throated roar of a home crowd. Every other national team manager envies what 130,000 cheering Scots can do to their side at Hampden. Before the tournament started when I spoke to Billy Bingham, the Irish team manager, he remembered that it was over 35 years since his country had won in Glasgow. "The Hampden roar is always worth a goal or two start to the Scots," he said ruefully: "That's the first thing we have to overcome."

And what happened? Thanks to a torrential rainstorm, and a rail strike, over 123,000 moral supporters the Scots team expected preferred to stay at home and watch the game on television. Only 7,483 people dotted the vast Hampden terraces when the game began. "It was," said the great-hearted Scots skipper Billy Bremner, "like playing in a floodlit mortuary." The absence of the roar was worth a goal to Ireland—and they quickly took it, Eric McMordie heading home the rebound from a shot by Georgie Best in the eleventh minute.

So the Scots faced another fight-back, this time on a swimming-pool of a pitch which defied all the delicate on-the-ground passing for which Scots are renowned. It was hard slog all the way until the golden head of Colin Stein got a richly deserved draw.

And the English? Well, they were set back on their heels at the start and had not Keith Newton's boot and Bobby Moore's head got in the way of two great centres from Colin Stein they would have been in more trouble than they bargained.

Even two English goals in four minutes failed to dampen the Scottish hopes. They never tamed Willie Henderson—and that great, great header from Stein just before the interval must have sent them in at half-time for a roasting from Sir Alf Ramsey.

So the championship was not to be—but still the Scots had plenty of heroes. Tommy Lawrence — gallantly carrying on against the Welsh, although concussed, and his replacement, Jim Herriot holding nearly everything the rampant Irish could throw at him. Eddie McCreadie who alone took on the job at least three Englishmen had found enough for them—holding the irrepressible George Best. Pat Stanton, who cleared a "certain" Irish goal with immense calm, and Billy McNeill who dominated in the air and also showed the whizz-kid English forwards that he knew a thing or two about ground play as well. And, of course, the little dynamo himself, Billy Bremner, who played a real captain's game in all three matches and time and again forced his colleagues back into the game when all seemed lost.

Up front, unselfish Alan Gilzean, who took most of the punishment so that Colin Stein could get the chances—and how well the golden boy took those that came his way! Willie Henderson, dazzling and bemusing the English with his will-o'-the-wisp dribbles and so nearly crowning a great Wembley display with an even greater goal.

Last, but not least, the young debutante Eddie Gray—yet another of a long line of Scots who have made their first international appearance in the cauldron of an England-

SCOTLAND versus ENGLAND

A clash of captains. This time Billy Bremner wins the duel with England's Bobby Moore

Scotland affair and who have gone on to greater glories. Gray looks destined to repeat his fine Wembley performance more than once in the future—and Scotland are surely destined to see him more often on the winning side in doing it.

131

Scots on the attack—and England 'keeper Banks makes a spectacular save

John Greig does well to clear Bobby Charlton's low header

Now it's tragedy for Greig. He trips Martin Peters. It's a penalty for England . . . and goalkeeper Herriot has no chance to stop Hurst's fierce shot from the spot for England's third goal

133

SCOTLAND'S PICTURE-BOOK GOAL

*Scotland, sad to say, manage only one goal at Wembley —
but it comes straight out of the picture-book. It is a header
from Stein (centre) which foxes Banks and the rest of the
England defence. Gilzean is on the right*

SCOTLAND versus IRELAND

Billy Bremner is a tower of strength in defence. Always on the spot, always working, he leaps high to head away a well-placed ball from Dougan. Scotland breathes again at Hampden

137

SCOTLAND VERSUS WALES

138

A goal for Scotland at Wrexham. The scorer is Stein. It´s a shot from 10 yards out which the Welsh defender Burton cannot stop

Goalkeeper Lawrence clutches at the empty air. The ball is past him—and Ron Davies has scored the first goal to Wales

Wanted— a British Cup!

by SIR ROBERT KELLY

(Chairman, Celtic)

EUROPEAN COMPETITIONS such as the Champions' Cup, Cup Winners' Cup and Fairs Cup, have created great interest in recent years and, while they have provided many exciting and entertaining games, I find they have one major drawback. That is the fact that ties are decided on the home and away principal. This system has produced defensive football which is frustrating to the players and annoying to the fans.

I have been campaigning for a number of years for a British Cup, made up of the top eight teams in England and the top eight in Scotland and played on a knock-out basis. Such a competition would require only four playing days to finish. I think it would provide some wonderful games and prove much more lucrative to the smaller clubs because the expenses would be considerably less than any team has to meet in a European event.

Another point in favour of this idea is that it would stimulate the League competition. More teams would have something to play for in the closing weeks of the season and one imagines there could be quite a struggle to earn one of the Cup places. Clubs who found they couldn't quite earn a place in Europe might have the consolation of appearing in the British Cup.

The whole outlook on football has changed drastically in the last decade and it is still changing. The game at the top has become a grim, serious business and a great deal of the enjoyment which spectators, players and managers shared has gone altogether. The undue emphasis on winning, sometimes at any price, is one of the principal reasons. Another is the undisciplined and unsportsmanlike conduct of many players. This attitude springs from the World Cup in Switzerland in 1958. Hungary and Brazil met in a semi-final which erupted into a real battle, both on and off the field. The conduct of both teams was so disgraceful that I considered that both countries should have been barred from the competition. However, this action was not taken by F.I.F.A., the ruling body. Consequently things have become progressively worse.

We see behaviour in the highest class of football that is not tolerated in the minor grades. I feel that the higher the standard, the better the conduct should be. If a player has the ability to attain international rank it should be up to him to conduct himself in a manner worthy of the honour.

In this connection, I do not think the game is any more robust than in former years; it is a game of physical contact in which hard knocks are unavoidable. The big change is in the attitude of the players, many of whom apparently cannot accept the knocks without wanting to retaliate. This always leads to trouble, both on the field and on the terracing. We have had in recent years the very disturbing feature of players exaggerating and even feigning injuries in order to gain an advantage.

It is of paramount importance for the good of the game that clubs and authorities do everything possible to encourage a higher standard of sportsmanship among all players so that the most crucial match can be played robustly but within the rules.

Referees and refereeing have come in for a good deal of criticism. Most of it, I feel, is unjustified. It should be remembered that players who show dissent and harass the man in charge are not helping him in his difficult duty and may cause him to make mistakes which could have been avoided if he had been able to concentrate on his job. As to the recruiting of referees, I think it is a great pity that more ex-players of good reputation do not join the ranks. Football is one of the few sports which does not utilise past performers. I suggested some years ago that clubs should put forward the names of players whom they considered as suitable. It would be a necessary qualification that any applicant had a good record during his playing career. In order to attract applications, I think the salary would have to be on a par with their earnings as players—and I would employ them on a full-time basis.

It does seem odd to me that on a big match-day the referee, who has an extremely responsible role, is paid only a fraction of what the other participants are earning.

Whatever may be said about football in Scotland, the great success of Celtic in the past few seasons underlines the fact that we produce players equal to, if not better than, any other country in the world. Celtic were the first British team to win the European Cup and also the only team to have done so with players of one nationality. This was a remarkable achievement when one considers the relatively small population of Scotland compared to that of England or any of the large countries on the Continent.

Backbone of the English League—the Scot!

by DOUG GARDNER

(World Sports)

IF THE ENGLISH LEAGUE is the hardest in world soccer to win—and no other has as many teams battling for its titles—then the Sassenachs ought to thank the Scots for making it so. Without the men from north of the Border there might not be any English League at all.

It's been going on ever since soccer was first organised in England. When the first four unofficial internationals were played between the two countries in the 1870s, the entire Scottish teams were selected from London-based players. At least half Manager Bobby Brown's World Cup squad last season were "Anglos". All but two or three of the twenty-two English First Division clubs last season had a stack of Scots on their books—and it's no coincidence that those with the most finished on top of the heap.

Leeds United snapped up fiery Billy Bremner while he was still in schools soccer in Falkirk. He has since won every possible international honour for Scotland and last season captained Leeds to the League title. Behind him, talking with the same accent: Glasgow-born Eddie Gray, a new international, Peter Lorimer, from Dundee, and Wally Sweeney and Jimmy Lumsden, both from Glasgow.

Look at the League's other front-runners last season: Liverpool, managed by Scot Bill Shankly, with goalkeeper

Tommy Lawrence and iron-man Ron Yeats, from Aberdeen, at the heart of one of the best defences in the country. Would the Arsenal defence also be as feared as it is without Ayr-born Ian Ure—a £72,000 bargain from Dundee—or skipper Frank McLintock?

Remove Dundee's Charlie Cooke and Motherwell's John Boyle from the build-up and you have a hole in Chelsea's midfield big enough to sink Ben Nevis. And, of course, Eddie McCreadie has long been a mainstay of the defence.

Manchester United, despite their comparatively poor form in the League last season, is still the most famous club outside Britain; recognised and feared for their football from Moscow to Montevideo and with a record in Europe second to none. Who put them there? It was a Scot: manager Sir Matt Busby. And his line-ups have always been noted for a strong Scottish accent. The fame of such as Denis Law and Pat Crerand has spread far and wide in the years they have spent in Manchester United's service. Now there are equally skilful youngsters brought down from Scotland to refresh the United team, including Aberdeen-born John Fitzpatrick, Jimmy Ryan from Stirling and Willie Morgan from Glasgow.

The balding, canny head of Alan Gilzean has set up innumerable chances for the League's leading goal-scorer Jimmy Greaves to find the net; and it was a Jimmy Robertson goal, fashioned in Glasgow by way of St. Mirren, that won Spurs the F.A. Cup a few years back. Bob McKinlay has for years been a staunch centre-half for Nottingham Forest, where the stylish play of wing-half Jim Baxter also made its mark. Baxter first moved south to Sunderland, where they have nearly always had a whole crew of Scots—last season including half-back George Kinnell, who was born in Cowden-beath, Ralph Brand and Albert Brown from Edinburgh, George Herd of Glasgow, and George Mulhall from Aberdeen.

Some of the key Scots in other First Division clubs last season were West Ham's goalkeeper Bobby Ferguson; West Brom's Bobby Hope, the ex-Everton star Jimmy Gabriel at Southampton, and centre-forward Jim McCalliog at Sheffield Wednesday.

Would there be any First Division left if that lot were removed? Just imagine the panic-buying that would go on in the oh-so-English English League!

Of course, if you took all the Scots out of the other three divisions as well, there might not be anybody worthwhile to buy. Who has been the inspiration behind Derby County's promotion? Why, "Old Man" Dave Mackay, the player with a heart as big as his native Edinburgh—and voted by the English soccer scribes as joint Footballer of the Year. Then again, John McCormick, born in Glasgow, helped Crystal Palace into the First Division.

Watford have been glad to have goalkeeper Bob Slater of Musselburgh to help them up from the Third to the Second Division, to say nothing of star scorer Brian Scullion from Bo'ness. Luton were running them close with the former Partick goalkeeper Bill Taylor, Lanark-born Max Dougan, Fred Jardine of Dundee and Paisley-born Bill McDermott on their books. And the ex-Rangers forward Willie Penman proved a bargain buy at £10,000 for League-Cup winning Swindon Town.

In the Fourth Division? Well, look at the front-runners there: Doncaster with Bob Gilfillan of Cowdenbeath, Aberdeen's Lew Thom at Lincoln, and at Colchester Denis Mochan of Falkirk.

Makes you wonder why they have the cheek to call it the *English* League at all, doesn't it?

The sad story of the Fairs Cup

At one time Rangers' excursion into the Inter-Cities Fairs Cup competition which took them into the semi-final seemed very likely to provide the fillip they so badly needed. But it was not to be. Instead, it was Newcastle United who qualified to meet Ujpest Dozsa of Budapest in the final tie. To add insult to injury, a mob of Scottish hooligans left their ugly marks on the contest. . . .

The sad story began at Ibrox in the first leg of the semi-final against the moderately placed English First Division side. Rangers should have built a substantial lead. They had two-thirds of the play and a hatful of scoring chances, yet the result was a goalless draw. They even missed a penalty.

Rangers were tied down by a tight and tough Newcastle defence in which goalkeeper McFaul played magnificently. Not only did he save that penalty from Penman in the 34th minute, but he stopped certain-looking goals from Henderson, Jackson, Stein and a sizzling shot from Penman. And Newcastle returned home with the advantage for the all-important second leg.

From the outset this second match eight days later did not augur well for the Scots. Hours before the kick-off at St. James's Park misguided Rangers fans roamed through the streets of Newcastle singing, waving banners and holding up traffic. . . .

The game was a hard one, packed with tension from the first whistle. Ironically, it was two Scots who scored the goals which gave Newcastle victory. After 53 minutes, Scott, a former Hibernian player, beat Neef with a finely angled shot. Then with 12 minutes to go, Sinclair put a pile-driver into the top of the net.

THE FIRST LEG: The black-and-white shirted men of Newcastle, half-backs Moncur and Gibb, are desperate to clear the ball away from the menacing head of Stein and the waiting Persson

It's a penalty for Rangers. Goalkeeper McFaul has brought down Orjan Persson on the edge of the area. Andy Penman **(top right)** *takes the vital kick but McFaul* **(bottom right)** *anticipates its direction to bring off a superb save*

It was this second goal which sent the Scottish rowdies spilling on to the pitch. These were no friends of Glasgow Rangers. For 17 vicious minutes the hooligans fought and struggled. Slowly the police cleared the field and eventually the teams trooped back from their dressing-rooms. The game was finally played out without further interruption from the crowd.

It was a sad and sorry night.

150

*Newcastle United lead Rangers 2—0 with 10 minutes to go when the terraces at St. James's Park erupt. Brawling supporters from Glasgow invade the pitch and run wild. Both teams return to the dressing-rooms—that's Greig walking off **(bottom right)**, while the police quell the riot and the injured tend each other*

The North Sea invasion

EVERY FOOTBALL MANAGER dreams of picking up star players at bargain prices, but for one all-action, publicity-minded team boss, the dream turned into reality. It was Hal Stewart, the Morton manager, who had a brainwave in 1964. Why not barge into the amateur market in Denmark and beat other Continental countries for the personality players?

Goalkeeper Erik Sorensen was the first import and the deal was like an MI5 operation, for the player's identity and whereabouts remained on the secret list. The man in black was called Mr. X and the spectacular, blond-haired 'keeper was unmasked in a blaze of newspaper headlines.

Morton cornered the market at the time, but Dundee United moved in by spreading the search to Sweden. Other clubs were soon copying the trail-blazers.

It was good business for the Scottish clubs since the only fee paid out was the signing-on cheque to the players. The Scandinavians were happy at the new outlet for their talent and they were able to guarantee their future by collecting huge nest-eggs, sometimes soaring to the five-figure mark.

But not all the foreigners had to come to Scotland for security alone. Take Rangers' right-back Kaj Johansen, who was invited over by Sorensen to team up with him at Greenock. The two Danes became big favourites at

Acrobatic goalkeeping is a speciality with Bent Martin, the man Celtic signed from Aarhus after a European Cup Winner's Cup-tie

Finn Dossing, Dundee United's free scoring centre-forward from Denmark

Hearts went to Norway for Roald Jensen, an elegant inside-forward

Cappielow and Rangers paid around £20,000 to buy Johansen. Some time later he was followed by Sorensen, who was relegated to reserve football last season.

Johansen had taken a five-year business course in his native land and gone into an outfitter's business with a friend. It blossomed to such an extent that they employed a dozen assistants. Last summer the shop was sold for £56,000 because Kaj wanted to concentrate on the businesses he was building up in Glasgow. He bought a public-house and followed up by taking over a bar restaurant which he quickly modernised to suit present-day requirements. His next project promises to be a hotel in Stornoway. It is no accident that Johansen has been as successful off the field as on it. He speaks five languages and has a shrewd brain.

Morton have signed an entire team of Danes in five years but Hal Stewart cashed in a second time on his Scandinavians by selling the players to other Scottish clubs. Rangers signed

Erik Sorensen arrived in Scotland as Mr. X, Morton's big mystery signing in 1964

Carl Bertelsen was another Morton import. Later he moved to Dundee and Kilmarnock

Sorensen, Johansen and inside-forward Jorn Sorensen, who soon returned overseas; Carl Bertelsen, another of the pioneers, joined Dundee and then Kilmarnock; Hibs bought centre-half John Madsen.

And last season came the newest development. English clubs are not permitted to tap this source but once a player has lived in Scotland for two years, they can make a bid. The English League sanctioned the sale of wing-half Preben Arentoft to Newcastle United and a couple of weeks later Borge Thorup had switched to Crystal Palace.

If Morton paid out handsome sums to tempt these players into professionalism, they received far more in transfer fees—which must have totalled around £100,000. How precious that cash has been to Morton in their eternal financial strife!

Dundee United manager, Jerry Kerr, unearthed a scoring centre-forward with a Danish Second Division team. Finn Dossing proved a cracking tip-off. Manager Kerr was lucky

Johansen (left) gets down to the business of football and goes through a tough training routine with the Rangers

in Sweden, too. He saw wing-half Lennart Wing and left-winger Orjan Persson play for Oergryte against Dunfermline in the Fairs Cup and followed up his interest.

The international pair quit Gothenburg for Tayside and strengthened United's team in a big way. Big Mogens Berg was another signing from Denmark, but back trouble prevented him from making his mark. Wing returned to Sweden after two seasons to resume his job as a fireman and Persson was transferred to Rangers in a highly beneficial move.

Hearts went to Norway for their first Scandinavian, having seen winger Roald Jensen play against them for the Bergen club, Brann. He came with the reputation of scoring

After a training stint at Ibrox Johansen, a great favourite with fans of all ages, is cornered by a bunch of autograph hunters

500 goals in his own country but never managed to produce such goal-scoring magic for the Tynecastle team despite his elegant ball control. Jensen was joined last year by René Moller from Freja Randers in Denmark. The powerfully built centre-forward won himself a lucrative contract but lost his place after a promising start.

The other Norwegian to grace the Scottish scene briefly was Finn Seemann, a tricky winger from the Lyn club in Oslo. Now he is with DWS Amsterdam, who lost to Rangers in the Fairs Cup last season.

Aberdeen were early starters in the Danish talent race but they met with mixed success. Forwards Mortensen and Ravn were released when manager Eddie Turnbull took over at Pittodrie but half-back Jens Petersen proved a fine investment. He was captain of the Dons last season when he was joined in the mid-line by rugged Henning Boel, a Dane who had been in America.

The only other side to sign a foreigner was Celtic. They were so impressed by the wonderful goalkeeping of Bent Martin during a European Cup Winners' cup-tie against Aarhus that they arranged a date to fix the deal. However, Martin never made the grade at Celtic Park and joined Dunfermline for a small fee. There, he played in the 1968 Scottish Cup winning team.

Despite a new outlook by Dundee United, more players will flock to this country via Morton even if home-reared stars dislike the chunky cheques that the visitors pick up. As the Scots go south for the fat signing-on fees and bulky wage packets, so the Scandinavians will head in the Greenock direction.

Orjan Persson was spotted in a Fairs Cup-tie by Dundee United. Now the left-winger scores valuable goals for Rangers. This was a near-miss against Celtic

The bigger they are . . .

(or, how Berwick beat the Rangers)

IN THE NINETY-FIVE YEARS of the Scottish Cup tournament there have been countless shocks, yet one sensation stands out above all others—the day the mighty Glasgow Rangers were knocked out by Berwick Rangers. Fancy a Second Division team from England showing such disrespect to the great club over the Border!

Any Berwick man will rap out the date of the historic match without a moment's hesitation. It was 28 January, 1967—probably the blackest day in the illustrious life of the famous Light Blues.

Before the first round tie, Berwick player-manager Jock Wallace promised that there was a surprise in store for Rangers. Few people took the big goalkeeper very seriously but it was good propaganda for the attendance at compact Shielfield Park. Still, Jock could claim to be something of an expert in Cup upsets, for he had helped Hereford, a non-League club, to deliver a knock-out blow to Newcastle United.

This time he was the inspiration behind the wee Rangers 1–0 triumph. He was unbeatable in the home goal—and every other Berwick player was on top form, too.

But the glory of scoring that winning goal went to little

Berwick Rangers, heroes one and all. The men who shocked mighty Glasgow Rangers. Back row (left to right): G. Haig, J. Kilgannon, J. Wallace, R. Craig, I. Riddell, A. Rogers (substitute). Front row: T. Lumsden, K. Dowds, D. Coutts, G. Christie, S. Reid, A. Ainslie.

inside-forward Sammy Reid. Kenny Dowds and George Christie were involved in the build-up to the move which enabled Reid to shoot the ball past Norrie Martin.

What a moment that was for Sammy! His football career had seemed to be over when he crashed into the boundary wall during a game between Hibs and Clyde, his previous club, at Easter Road. He smashed his kneecap and the doctors inserted two pins into the knee. He was out of the game for eight months and it was a tribute to the surgery that he was able to make such a convincing comeback. Earlier in his career, he had played for Motherwell at the same time as Ian St. John who had then been transferred to Liverpool. But this was his finest memory of all.

Just after Reid's goal, centre-forward Christie had two

161

This is it. The goal that put Glasgow Rangers out of the Cup in the first round in 1967. Goalkeeper Martin is left floundering as a shot from Berwick's Sammy Reid whips past him into the net. It's the biggest upset for years

chances to increase the Berwick lead but Martin saved superbly on each occasion. The Berwick advantage was slender but it was enough.

Who made up the giant-killing outfit? Led by Wallace, they had Gordon Haig, ex-Raith Rovers, at right-back and Ian Riddell, from St. Mirren, at left-back. Russell Craig, a former Blantyre junior, Doug Coutts (Aberdeen) and Jim Kilgannon (East Stirling) made up the mid-line. Right-winger Tommy Lumsden was freed by Hearts and he partnered Reid. Centre-forward George Christie had signed from East Fife. There was little experience about the

Left: *Player-manager Jock Wallace was the man who directed the Berwick giant-killers. Here he is fulfilling his rôle as goalkeeper, saving the ball from the eager heads of McLean and Forrest, of Rangers. Haig (Berwick) stands guard on the line*

163

Here's joy and anguish: goal-scorer Sammy Reid is mobbed by Berwick Rangers players. A fan dashes on to the pitch. Goalkeeper Martin, however, can hardly believe it and lies disconsolate on the ground. There's a feeling of despair, too, for Glasgow Rangers' manager Symon and he and Bobby Seith bow their heads in defeat

left-wing pair: Ken Dowds had stepped up from junior club Arniston Rangers and Alan Ainslie had been spotted in schools football.

Rangers, on the other hand, had bought Kaj Johansen from Morton, Alex Smith from Dunfermline and George McLean from St. Mirren at an approximate cost of £100,000.

The cheers and the chanting last a long while and every Berwick Ranger receives his own special ovation. This is Gordon Haig being chaired off

The defeat signalled the end of the road for McLean and Forrest as Ibrox first team men. McLean went to Dundee in part exchange for Andy Penman and Forrest was sold to Preston.

Jock Wallace claims that his pre-match prediction was no gimmick:

"I expected to win because I had seen Rangers in one game against Aberdeen and I thought they were struggling fitness-wise. So I went back to my players and told them we could beat Rangers because we were the fitter team. For three weeks I drummed it into them. The psychology began to work.

"Don't forget we were in the middle of a winning run, having strung together eight victories. My theory was that Rangers would hammer us in the first 20 minutes, but if we could hold out, John Greig would move out of his own defence to help the forwards. That's exactly what happened and Berwick had four men upfield to exploit the gap."

In the middle of the most astonishing Cup upset of all time was Edinburgh referee Eddie Thomson, who says this:

"Before the match I was passing the time with Berwick centre-half Doug Coutts. He told me that his team would do well to hold Rangers to four or five goals. Ten minutes from the end the same player asked how long there was left to play and for the first time he realised a Berwick victory was possible. 'We could beat them', he gasped.

"Anxious Ibrox players wanted a time check, too, but the information didn't help them. Yes, it was no ordinary game, but one that had made history.

"It's hard to wear a smile after such a shock dismissal, so

Never before has there been a day such as this for the Berwick supporters. They invade the pitch to cheer their heroes when it's all over

it said a lot for skipper John Greig when he knocked at my door and thanked me for my control. He said: 'We have no complaints, we beat ourselves.' That was the gesture of a real sportsman."

What happened to Sammy Reid? He left Berwick for Dumbarton and quit the game the following year.

Berwick were not newcomers to the giant-killing business, for they had slammed Dundee 3–1 in the fifties. Dundee's worst defeat, however, was in the first round in 1959 when they lost 1–0 to the Highland League club Fraserburgh. Outside-right Strachan scored the only goal in the first half and the outsiders spent the rest of the time clinging to their golden lead. That Tayside team, managed by Willie Thornton, included Bill Brown, Alex Hamilton, Doug Cowie, Alan Cousin and Hugh Robertson.

Jubilant Fraserburgh officials presented each member of the Dundee team with a parting gift. But a box of fish apiece gave little consolation on that long, sad journey home.

'KEEPING WITH A PUNCH

Arbroath goalkeeper Jim Williamson punches clear
from the head of Dunfermline's Jim Frazer.

THE STORY OF
THE SEASON
1968-69

by JOHN RAFFERTY
(The Scotsman)

AGAIN the story of a Scottish football season became the story of Celtic. They won the League Championship for the fourth successive time, they brought their League Cup wins to four in a row and, when they shattered Rangers in the Scottish Cup final, they had once again made a clean sweep of the principal Scottish tournaments. For them there was but one bitter memory, and that was of the defensive mistake that caused them to be eliminated from the European Champions' Cup.

They had survived against A.C. Milan in a blizzard in San Siro Stadium and with a little more enterprise in the last quarter-hour they might have won; but they did not worry, for the Italians seemed at their mercy at Celtic Park in the second leg. Instead, a goal was gifted to Milan and Celtic on a bad night could not pull it back. So the grand slam was burst.

It took Celtic 34 weeks to win their championship. The final healthy lead hid some of the worry over the strain that began to show in a team that was playing its fourth tense season without a full close-season break. The pressure was put on solidly by losing twice to Rangers.

The cynical have said that Celtic and Rangers should play each other twice and that should be the League championship.

Often it works out this way—and never before have Rangers beaten their old rivals twice in a season and still lost the championship. These victories were unexpected, for Celtic had twice beaten them comfortably in the League Cup.

To Rangers' dismay they blundered quickly each time after beating Celtic, to throw away their advantage. They beat Celtic by a controversial 4–2 in their first League game but before the flush of victory had cooled Aberdeen were taking three goals off them at Ibrox Stadium and raising fresh cries for changes.

Colin Stein was bought from Hibs for £100,000 and was immediately a demi-god when he scored hat-tricks in successive games; Rangers were again swollen with hope but the next week they went to Paisley and, in the mist, on a frozen pitch, they were beaten by St Mirren, the shock team of the first half of the season.

Again Rangers had illusions of success when they beat Celtic by 1–0 on January 2. But in the next game they went to Kilmarnock and were beaten; to make matters worse Colin Stein was ordered off the field. Again their dreams were shattered. During this time Celtic kept going—and not another team was to beat them until the last week of the season when, on their celebration night, Morton were at Celtic Park and their Danish outside left, Bartram, scored a hat-trick in the first ten minutes.

The earlier challengers began to drop out until in the final run-in it was a straight contest between Celtic and Rangers. The newly promoted club, St Mirren, had stuck courageously close to the top until the weakness in reserve strength took its inevitable toll. Kilmarnock under their bright new manager, Walter McCrae, asserted themselves. But something more than inspired direction was needed. Still, in their centenary year theirs was a commendable effort; they finished ten points up on the previous season.

George Farm at Dunfermline roared a belligerent challenge. Right up to the last week of the season his team had a chance of being runners-up in the championship. They would probably have achieved that, to Rangers embarrassment, had they not been so disconsolate over being roughly eliminated from the European Cup Winners Cup in the semi-final tie in Bratislava.

Dundee United, too, settled to a sound co-ordinated game which had them ready winners and made Tannadice a dreaded field. They kept within striking distance of the leaders throughout, and, at least, had the satisfaction of finishing the season with the top goal-scorer in Kenny Cameron. But as the struggle to hold high estate in the League was kept going by those who sought a place in next season's Fairs Cities Cup, a surprise new challenger loomed from an unlikely quarter—Perth.

St. Johnstone had not been taken seriously, but they sold McDonald to Rangers for £50,000 and for less than half that amount Willie Ormond bought Henry Hall—and almost overnight revitalised the team. Only Celtic were more consistent in the latter half of the season and they finished in sixth place in the League with Hall the second top goal-scorer in the country.

Meanwhile, Celtic were saving games in spectacular fashion. With 11 minutes to go on a muddy field at Tannadice they were being held to 1–1 by Dundee United, but won by 3–1. With 12 minutes to go at Easter Road Hibs led them 2–1, but Hughes came storming into the middle and Celtic won 5–2. At Perth they were down 2–0 at half-time and Hughes had been taken off injured—but they won in injury time and Stein was later to say that that match won the championship. Again, they were 2–0 down to Kilmarnock and equalised in injury time. Tremendous fitness was shown in these stirring recoveries.

The final blow to Rangers was the fourth ordering-off of Colin Stein in the last minute of a match against Clyde which Rangers were winning by 6–0 and in which Stein had scored three goals. He was suspended till the end of the season and so missed the cup final.

At the bottom of the league Raith Rovers, when relegation loomed, appointed a new manager, Jimmy Millar, once of Rangers, and he stiffened the team and won a vital match at Falkirk between the clubs most deeply involved. Falkirk, also with a new manager—Willie Cunningham—went down along with Arbroath, who had toiled throughout the season. Motherwell had all along led the second division and Ally McLeod brought his Ayr United with a late run to join them in promotion.

Abroad, the name of Scotland was proudly upheld. Celtic went to the quarter-final of the Champions Cup; Dunfermline to the semi-final of the Cup Winners Cup and Rangers to the semi-final of the Fairs Cities Cup. In Cyprus the national team impressively scored five goals in a qualifying match for the World Cup finals.

The story of the national team was one of frustration for the team manager Bobby Brown, as he tried to get a pool of players training together on club lines and found the heavy club commitments making this impossible. The draw against West Germany at Hampden when Bobby Murdoch equalised with a great goal was only half satisfactory as it sends Scotland looking for wins in Austria and Germany.

It was, all through, an encouraging season with attendances overall up; in Celtic's case their League attendances were the highest in the history of the club. There was just one dull spot in Edinburgh, where Hibs toppled after two disappointing results, and Hearts struggled all season with forwards who could not score goals.

The 1968–69 SEASON
All the facts and figures

THE END-OF-SEASON TABLES

DIVISION 1

	P	HOME W	D	L	F	A	AWAY W	D	L	F	A	P
Celtic	34	12	3	2	50	19	11	5	1	39	13	54
Rangers ..	34	13	3	1	47	12	8	4	5	34	20	49
Dunfermline ..	34	12	4	1	42	20	7	3	7	21	25	45
Kilmarnock ..	34	10	6	1	30	15	5	8	4	20	17	44
Dundee United	34	12	3	2	40	25	5	6	6	21	24	43
St. Johnstone ..	34	11	2	4	39	22	5	3	9	27	37	37
Airdrieonians ..	34	10	5	2	27	16	3	6	8	19	28	37
Hearts	34	7	7	3	26	20	7	1	9	26	34	36
Dundee ..	34	4	8	5	24	23	6	4	7	23	25	32
Morton ..	34	8	5	4	34	27	4	3	10	24	41	32
St. Mirren ..	34	7	4	6	24	21	4	6	7	16	33	32
Hibernian ..	34	9	2	6	38	24	3	5	9	22	35	31
Clyde	34	6	7	4	20	18	3	6	8	15	32	31
Partick Thistle	34	7	3	7	21	24	2	7	8	18	29	28
Aberdeen ..	34	6	5	6	26	24	3	3	11	24	35	26
Raith Rovers ..	34	6	2	9	23	29	2	3	12	22	38	21
Falkirk ..	34	4	6	7	21	27	1	2	14	12	42	18
Arbroath ..	34	4	3	10	24	34	1	3	13	17	48	16

compiled by
HARRY SPRINGATE

DIVISION 2

	P		HOME					AWAY				P
		W	D	L	F	A	W	D	L	F	A	
Motherwell ..	36	16	2	0	68	12	14	2	2	44	11	64
Ayr United ..	36	13	3	2	54	15	10	4	4	28	16	53
East Fife	36	13	4	1	51	14	8	2	8	31	31	48
Stirling Albion	36	11	4	3	41	19	10	2	6	26	21	48
Queen of the South	36	11	2	5	43	20	9	5	4	32	21	47
Forfar Athletic	36	10	4	4	42	26	8	3	7	29	30	43
Albion Rovers	36	13	2	3	37	18	6	3	9	23	38	43
Stranraer ..	36	10	3	5	28	15	7	4	7	29	30	41
East Stirling ..	36	12	1	5	42	21	5	4	9	28	41	39
Montrose ..	36	11	2	5	35	20	4	2	12	24	51	34
Queen's Park ..	36	8	3	7	25	26	5	4	9	25	33	33
Cowdenbeath ..	36	5	3	10	32	37	7	2	9	22	30	29
Clydebank ..	36	4	7	7	28	30	2	8	8	24	37	27
Dumbarton ..	36	7	2	9	33	35	4	3	11	13	34	27
Hamilton A. ..	36	4	6	8	24	33	4	2	12	13	39	24
Berwick Rangers	36	6	6	6	24	24	1	3	14	18	46	23
Brechin City ..	36	6	3	9	25	33	2	3	13	15	45	22
Alloa Athletic	36	4	3	11	23	31	3	4	11	22	48	21
Stenhousemuir	36	5	3	10	30	42	1	3	14	25	83	18

The Scottish Cup 1968–69

FIRST ROUND			SECOND ROUND			THIRD ROUND		
Celtic	3:	8	Celtic	0:	3			
Partick T.	3:*	1				Celtic		3
Motherwell	1:	1	Clyde	0:*	0			
Clyde	1:	2						
East Stirling		2	East Stirling	1:	0			
Stirling A.		0				St. Johnstone		2
St. Johnstone		3	St. Johnstone	1:	3			
Arbroath		2						
Dundee Utd.		2	Dundee Utd.		6			
Queen's Park		1				Dundee Utd.		2
Ayr Utd.		1	Ayr Utd.		2			
Queen of the South		0						
Stranraer		3	Stranraer		1			
East Fife		1				Morton		3
Falkirk		1	Morton		3			
Morton		2						
Aberdeen		3	Aberdeen	2:	2			
Berwick R.		0				Aberdeen	0:	3
Raith R.		0	Dunfermline	2:	0			
Dunfermline		2						
Montrose		1	Montrose	1:	1			
Cowdenbeath		0				Kilmarnock	0:	0
Kilmarnock		6	Kilmarnock	1:	4			
Glasgow Univ.		0						
Stenhousemuir		0	Airdrieonians	1:	3			
Airdrieonians		3				Airdrieonians		0
Dumbarton		0	St. Mirren	1:	1			
St. Mirren		1						
Dundee		1	Hearts		0			
Hearts		2				Rangers		*1
Hibernian		0	Rangers		*2			
Rangers		*1						

* *Home team*

FIRST PRELIMINARY ROUND

Alloa A. 6 Ross Co. 1; Brechin C. 1: 2 Montrose 1:3;
Cowdenbeath 1 Clydebank 0; Forfar 1 Nairn Co. 2;
St. Cuthberts 1 Civil Service 0.

—how Celtic carried it off

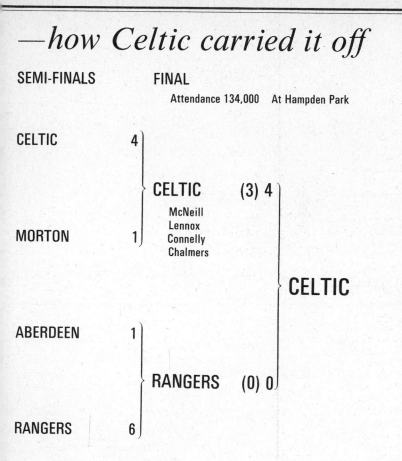

SEMI-FINALS

FINAL

Attendance 134,000   At Hampden Park

CELTIC 4

CELTIC (3) 4
McNeill
Lennox
Connelly
Chalmers

MORTON 1

CELTIC

ABERDEEN 1

RANGERS (0) 0

RANGERS 6

SECOND PRELIMINARY ROUND

Alloa A. 0 : 1 East Stirling 0 : 2 ; Dumbarton 3 Vale of Leithen 2 ;
Glasgow Univ. 5 St. Cuthberts 2 ; Hamilton A. 0 Cowdenbeath 2 ;
Montrose 6 Fraserburgh 1 ; Nairn Co. 0 Berwick R. 2 ;
Stenhousemuir 1 Albion R. 0 ; Stranraer 2 Elgin C. 0

Scottish League Cup 1968–69

Quarter Final Round (First Leg)

Ayr United	0	Clyde	1
Celtic	10	Hamilton A.	0
East Fife	1	Hibernian	4
Stranraer	0	Dundee	4

Quarter Final Round (Second Leg)

Clyde	2	Ayr United	0
(Clyde won 3–0 on aggregate)			
Dundee	6	Stranraer	0
(Dundee won 10–0 on aggregate)			
Hamilton A.	2	Celtic	4
(Celtic won 14–2 on aggregate)			
Hibernian	2	East Fife	1
(Hibernian won 6–2 on aggregate)			

Semi-finals

Celtic	1	Clyde	0
Hibernian	2	Dundee	1

Final

Celtic	6	Hibernian	2

Scottish League Champions

FIRST DIVISION

1892–3	Celtic
1893–4	Celtic
1894–5	Hearts
1895–6	Celtic
1896–7	Hearts
1897–8	Celtic
1898–9	Rangers
1899–1900	Rangers
1900–1	Rangers
1901–2	Rangers
1902–3	Hibernian
1903–4	Third Lanark
1904–5	Celtic
1905–6	Celtic
1906–7	Celtic
1907–8	Celtic
1908–9	Celtic
1909–10	Celtic
1910–11	Rangers
1911–12	Rangers
1912–13	Rangers
1913–14	Celtic
1914–15	Celtic
1915–16	Celtic
1916–17	Celtic
1917–18	Rangers
1918–19	Celtic
1919–20	Rangers
1920–1	Rangers
1921–2	Celtic
1922–3	Rangers
1923–4	Rangers
1924–5	Rangers
1925–6	Celtic
1926–7	Rangers
1927–8	Rangers
1928–9	Rangers
1929–30	Rangers
1930–1	Rangers
1931–2	Motherwell
1932–3	Rangers
1933–4	Rangers
1934–5	Rangers
1935–6	Celtic
1936–7	Rangers
1937–8	Celtic
1938–9	Rangers

1946–7	Rangers	1929–30	Leith Athletic
1947–8	Hibernian	1930–1	Third Lanark
1948–9	Rangers	1931–2	East Stirling
1949–50	Rangers	1932–3	Hibernian
1950–1	Hibernian	1933–4	Albion Rovers
1951–2	Hibernian	1934–5	Third Lanark
1952–3	Rangers	1935–6	Falkirk
1953–4	Celtic	1936–7	Ayr United
1954–5	Aberdeen	1937–8	Raith Rovers
1955–6	Rangers	1938–9	Cowdenbeath
1956–7	Rangers	1946–7	Dundee
1957–8	Hearts	1947–8	East Fife
1958–9	Rangers	1948–9	Raith Rovers
1959–60	Hearts	1949–50	Morton
1960–1	Rangers	1950–1	Q. of the South
1961–2	Dundee	1951–2	Clyde
1962–3	Rangers	1952–3	Stirling Albion
1963–4	Rangers	1953–4	Motherwell
1964–5	Kilmarnock	1954–5	Airdrie
1965–6	Celtic	1955–6	Queen's Park
1966–7	Celtic	1956–7	Clyde
1967–8	Celtic	1957–8	Stirling Albion
1968–9	Celtic	1958–9	Ayr United
		1959–60	St. Johnstone

SECOND DIVISION

1921–2	Alloa	1960–1	Stirling Albion
1922–3	Queen's Park	1961–2	Clyde
1923–4	St. Johnstone	1962–3	St. Johnstone
1924–5	Dundee U.	1963–4	Morton
1925–6	Dunfermline	1964–5	Stirling Albion
1926–7	Bo'ness	1965–6	Ayr United
1927–8	Ayr United	1966–7	Morton
1928–9	Dundee U.	1967–8	St. Mirren
		1968–9	Motherwell

Scottish Cup Winners

1873–4	Queen's Park	1904–5	Third Lanark
1874–5	Queen's Park	1905–6	Hearts
1875–6	Queen's Park	1906–7	Celtic
1876–7	Vale of Leven	1907–8	Celtic
1877–8	Vale of Leven	1908–9	*Cup withheld*
1878–9	Vale of Leven		*due to riot*
1879–80	Queen's Park	1909–10	Dundee
1880–1	Queen's Park	1910–11	Celtic
1881–2	Queen's Park	1911–12	Celtic
1882–3	Dumbarton	1912–13	Falkirk
1883–4	Queen's Park	1913–14	Celtic
1884–5	Renton	1914–19	*Competition*
1885–6	Queen's Park		*suspended*
1886–7	Hibernian	1919–20	Kilmarnock
1887–8	Renton	1920–1	Partick T.
1888–9	Third Lanark	1921–2	Morton
1889–90	Queen's Park	1922–3	Celtic
1890–1	Hearts	1923–4	Airdrie
1891–2	Celtic	1924–5	Celtic
1892–3	Queen's Park	1925–6	St. Mirren
1893–4	Rangers	1926–7	Celtic
1894–5	St. Bernard's	1927–8	Rangers
1895–6	Hearts	1928–9	Kilmarnock
1896–7	Rangers	1929–30	Rangers
1897–8	Rangers	1930–1	Celtic
1898–9	Celtic	1931–2	Rangers
1899–1900	Celtic	1932–3	Celtic
1900–1	Hearts	1933–4	Rangers
1901–2	Hibernian	1934–5	Rangers
1902–3	Rangers	1935–6	Rangers
1903–4	Celtic	1936–7	Celtic

1937–8	East Fife	1956–7	Falkirk
1938–9	Clyde	1957–8	Clyde
1939–40	*Competition*	1958–9	St. Mirren
	suspended	1959–60	Rangers
1946–7	Aberdeen	1960–1	Dunfermline
1947–8	Rangers	1961–2	Rangers
1948–9	Rangers	1962–3	Rangers
1949–50	Rangers	1963–4	Rangers
1950–1	Celtic	1964–5	Celtic
1951–2	Motherwell	1965–6	Rangers
1952–3	Rangers	1966–7	Celtic
1953–4	Celtic	1967–8	Dunfermline
1954–5	Clyde	1968–9	Celtic
1955–6	Hearts		

*In 1878–9 Vale of Leven were awarded the
Cup, Rangers failing to appear.
In 1883–4 Queen's Park were awarded the
Cup, Vale of Leven failing to appear.*

Scottish League Cup Winners

1945–6	Aberdeen	1957–8	Celtic
1946–7	Rangers	1958–9	Hearts
1947–8	East Fife	1959–60	Hearts
1948–9	Rangers	1960–1	Rangers
1949–50	East Fife	1961–2	Rangers
1950–1	Motherwell	1962–3	Hearts
1951–2	Dundee	1963–4	Rangers
1952–3	Dundee	1964–5	Rangers
1953–4	East Fife	1965–6	Celtic
1954–5	Hearts	1966–7	Celtic
1955–6	Aberdeen	1967–8	Celtic
1956–7	Celtic	1968–9	Celtic

Home International Championship 1968–69

WALES   (2) **3** **SCOTLAND** (2) **5**
Davies, R. 2   McNeill, Stein, Gilzean,
Toshack   Bremner, McLean

Attendance 18,765   (At Wrexham)

(1876–1969: Matches played 82; Scotland won 50; Wales won 15; Drawn 17)

N. IRELAND (0) **1** **ENGLAND**   (1) **3**
McMordie   Peters, Lee, Hurst (*penalty*)

Attendance 23,000   (At Windsor Park, Belfast)

(1882–1969: Matches played 76; England won 59; Ireland won 5; Drawn 12)

SCOTLAND   (0) **1** **N. IRELAND** (1) **1**
Stein   McMordie

Attendance 7,843   (At Hampden Park)

(1884–1969: Matches played 74; Scotland won 53; Ireland won 10; Drawn 11)

ENGLAND (0) **2** **WALES** (1) **1**
Charlton, R., Lee   Davies, R.

Attendance 70,000   (At Wembley)

(1879–1969: Matches played 79; England won 53;
Wales won 11; Drawn 15)

ENGLAND (2) **4** **SCOTLAND** (1) **1**
Peters 2   Stein
Hurst 2 (1 *penalty*)

Attendance 100,000   (At Wembley)

(1872–1969: Matches played 86; Scotland won 35;
England won 30; Drawn 21)

N. IRELAND (0) **0** **WALES** (0) **0**

Attendance 12,500   (At Windsor Park, Belfast)

(1882–1969: Matches played 75; Wales won 36;
Ireland won 23; Drawn 16)

FINAL TABLE

	P	W	D	L	F	A	P
England	3	3	0	0	9	3	6
Scotland	3	1	1	1	7	8	3
Ireland	3	0	2	1	2	4	2
Wales	3	0	1	2	4	7	1

World Cup 1970

EUROPE GROUP 7 – *Austria, Cyprus, West Germany, Scotland*

QUALIFYING COMPETITION:

1968

May 19	**Austria**	7	**Cyprus**	1
October 13	**Austria**	0	**W. Germany**	2
November 6	**Scotland** (1)	2	**Austria** (1)	1
	Law, Bremner		Starek	
November 23	**Cyprus**	0	**W. Germany**	1
December 11	**Cyprus** (0)	0	**Scotland** (5)	5
			Gilzean 2, Stein, Murdoch, Theodorou (*o.g.*)	

1969

April 16	**Scotland** (0)	1	**W. Germany** (1)	1
	Murdoch		Mueller	
April 19	**Cyprus**	1	**Austria**	2
May 10	**W. Germany**	1	**Austria**	0
May 17	**Scotland** (3)	8	**Cyprus** (0)	0
	Stein 4, Gray, McNeill, Henderson, Gemmell (*penalty*)			
May 21	**W. Germany**	12	**Cyprus**	0

To be played:

October 8	*W. Germany* . . .	*Scotland* . . .
November 5	*Austria* . . .	*Scotland* . . .

HOW THEY STAND

	P	W	D	L	F	A	P
WEST GERMANY	5	4	1	0	17	1	9
SCOTLAND	4	3	1	0	16	2	7
AUSTRIA	5	2	0	3	10	7	4
CYPRUS	6	0	0	6	2	35	0

YOUR TEAM'S
RESULTS AT
A GLANCE

On the pages beginning overleaf are all the match results of the 1968–69 season in the League, the Scottish Cup and Scottish League Cup. The results show the score of the club first, then follows **H** or **A** to indicate a home or away game; next, the identification number of the opponents. The respective cup matches are shown by the abbreviations **SC** (Scottish Cup) or **SLC** (Scottish League Cup), with **SF** (semifinal) and **F** (final).

For instance, the first entry under Aberdeen signifies that in their first match they lost 1–4 away to Clyde in the Scottish League Cup.

For quick reference, the identifying numbers of the clubs are:

The complete score-card for the 1968–69 season

DIVISION ONE		DIVISION TWO	
Aberdeen	1	Albion Rovers	19
Airdrieonians	2	Alloa Athletic	20
Arbroath	3	Ayr United	21
Celtic	4	Berwick Rangers	22
Clyde	5	Brechin City	23
Dundee	6	Clydebank	24
Dundee United	7	Cowdenbeath	25
Dunfermline Athletic	8	Dumbarton	26
Falkirk	9	East Fife	27
Heart of Midlothian	10	East Stirling	28
Hibernian	11	Forfar Athletic	29
Kilmarnock	12	Hamilton Academicals	30
Morton	13	Montrose	31
Partick Thistle	14	Motherwell	32
Raith Rovers	15	Queen of the South	33
Rangers	16	Queen's Park	34
St. Johnstone	17	Stenhousemuir	35
St. Mirren	18	Stirling Albion	36
		Stranraer	37

DIVISION ONE

ABERDEEN   (1)

1–4A5SLC; 1–0H8SLC; 4–1H7SLC; 0–2H5SLC;
2–1A8SLC; 0–1A7SLC; 4–4A6; 2–0H17; 0–1H7; 1–2A4;
1–2H10; 0–1A14; 0–1H5; 3–2A16; 2–1H15; 0–1A13;
2–2H3; 2–0H18; 1–5A8; 2–6H11; 0–2A2; 2–0H9;
1–2A12; 0–0H6; 1–3A17; 4–1A7; 1–3H4; 2–3A10;
3–0H22SC; 1–1H14; 2–2H8SC; 2–0A8SC; 0–0H12SC;
3–0A12SC; 1–2A3; 2–1A18; 2–3A15; 1–6 16 SC(SF);
2–2H8; 1–1A11; 6–3H13; 3–1H2; 0–0H16; 0–1A9;
0–1H12; 1–1A5.

AIRDRIEONIANS   (2)

2–3H10SLC; 3–0A12SLC; 1–1A6SLC; 2–0A10SLC;
2–0H12SLC; 0–3H6SLC; 2–0H3; 1–2A9; 2–1H10;
0–3H6; 1–5A11; 2–2H13; 1–2A7; 1–1H18; 1–1A14;
0–1A5; 3–0H17; 2–2H8; 1–1A16; 0–2H12; 2–0H1;
2–1A15; 0–0H4; 1–1H9; 1–1A10; 1–1A6; 3–1H11;
3–0A35SC; 1–1A13; 1–1H18SC; 2–1A18; 3–1A18SC;
0–1A16SC; 1–0H5; 1–3A17; 2–1H14; 0–1A8; 3–2H16;
1–2A12; 1–3A1; 2–0H15; 2–2A4; 1–0H7; 2–0A3.

ARBROATH   (3)

2–1H36SLC; 1–1A25SLC; 1–1H21SLC; 0–1A36SLC;
2–0H25SLC; 1–3A21SLC; 0–2A2; 1–1H18; 1–5A13;
2–4A7; 1–2H12; 1–3A15; 1–2H6; 0–2A8; 1–5H16;
0–5H4; 2–2A1; 3–4H11; 2–2A9; 1–5A17; 2–2H14;
2–3H10; 1–2A18; 3–1H13; 3–1H7; 0–1A12; 2–3A17SC;
0–1H15; 0–3A6; 0–1H8; 1–7A4; 2–1H1; 0–2A16;
2–1A11; 1–3A5; 3–0H9; 1–2H17; 1–2A14; 2–2A10;
1–1H5; 0–2H2.

CELTIC   (4)

2–0A16SLC; 4–1H13SLC; 4–0H14SLC; 1–0H16SLC;
3–0A13SLC; 6–1A14SLC; 3–0A5; 10–0H30SLC; 2–4H16;
1–1A8; 4–2A30SLC; 2–1H1; 2–0H7; 1–0 5 SLC(SF);
1–0A10; 2–1H17; 1–1A13; 3–1H6; 5–0A3; 2–0H15;
4–0A14; 5–2A11; 5–0H18; 0–0A9; 1–1H12; 0–0A2;
5–0H5; 0–1A16; 3–1H8; 3–1A1; 3–1A17; 3–3A14SC;
8–1H14SC; 5–0H10; 0–0A5SC; 3–0H5SC; 3–2H17SC;
7–1H3; 3–1A15; 1–0H14; 4–1 13 SC(SF); 1–1H11;
3–0A18; 3–2A17; 6–2 11 SLC(F); 5–2H9; 2–2H2;
2–2A12; 4–0 16 SC(F); 2–4H13; 2–1A6.

CLYDE   (5)

4–1H1SLC; 3–2A7SLC; 1–2A8SLC; 2–0A1SLC;
0–4H7SLC; 3–0H8SLC; 0–3H4; 1–0A21SLC; 0–4A14;
3–2H15; 2–0H21SLC; 0–0A17; 3–2A6; 0–1 4 SLC(SF);
1–1H11; 1–0A1; 2–0H9; 0–1A7; 1–0H2; 1–2A8; 1–1H16;
2–1H12; 3–2A10; 0–0H13; 0–1A18; 0–5A4; 1–2H14;
1–1A15; 0–3H17; 0–0H6; 1–1A32SC; 2–1H32SC;
1–2A11; 0–0H4SC; 3–3A9; 0–3A4SC; 0–1A2; 3–0H8;
2–2H7; 0–6A16; 3–1H3; 0–0A12; 0–1H10; 1–1A13;
0–0H18; 1–1A3; 1–1H1.

DUNDEE   (6)

4–0H12SLC; 1–2A10SLC; 1–1H2SLC; 2–2A12SLC;
4–0H10SLC; 3–0A2SLC; 4–4H1; 4–0A37SLC; 1–3A7;
2–3H17; 6–0H37SLC; 3–0A2; 2–3H5; 1–2 11 SLC(SF);
0–0H18; 2–1A3; 3–1H10; 1–3A4; 1–0H8; 1–0A9;
0–1A12; 1–1H14; 1–2A13; 0–0H11; 0–0A1; 1–2H7;
1–3A17; 1–1H2; 0–0A5; 1–2H10SC; 3–2A18; 3–0H3;
0–2A8; 0–0H9; 2–2A10; 0–0H12; 4–0A14; 2–2H15;
0–2H13; 3–1A11; 0–4A15; 3–2H16; 1–1A16; 1–2H4.

DUNDEE UNITED (7)

2–3A8SLC; 2–3H5SLC; 1–4A1SLC; 2–1H8SLC;
4–0A5SLC; 1–0H1SLC; 4–1A17; 3–1H6; 1–0A1; 4–2H3;
0–2A4; 0–3A12; 2–1H2; 1–1A11; 1–0H5; 2–1A15;
4–2H10; 2–0H13; 1–1A18; 2–1H9; 1–2A16; 2–1H14;
2–2A8; 4–2H17; 2–1A6; 1–4H1; 1–3A3; 1–3H4;
2–1H34SC; 2–2H12; 6–2H21SC; 2–3H13SC; 3–1H15;
0–1A10; 2–2A5; 2–1A13; 2–2H18; 2–2A9; 3–0H11;
2–1H16; 0–0A14; 2–2H8; 0–1A2.

DUNFERMLINE ATHLETIC (8)

3–2H7SLC; 0–1A1SLC; 2–1H5SLC; 1–2A7SLC;
1–2H1SLC; 0–3A5SLC; 3–2H15; 1–3A10; 1–1H4;
1–0A12; 3–1H17; 1–0A9; 0–3A16; 2–0H3; 5–3H13;
0–1A6; 2–1H5; 2–2A2; 5–1H1; 1–0A14; 6–2H18;
1–3A11; 2–2H7; 3–0A15; 4–2H10; 1–3A4; 1–1H12;
1–2A17; 2–0A15SC; 2–0H9; 1–0A3; 2–0A13; 2–2A1SC;
0–2H1SC; 2–0H6; 0–3A5; 1–0H2; 2–2A1; 2–0H14;
2–1A18; 2–2A7; 1–1H11; 0–3H16.

FALKIRK (9)

1–1H15SLC; 3–2A17SLC; 0–2A11SLC; 2–4A15SLC;
2–2H17SLC; 0–2H11SLC; 0–2A13; 2–1H2; 2–3A11;
0–2H18; 1–2A16; 0–1H8; 1–3H10; 0–2A5; 2–1H17;
1–5A12; 0–1H6; 1–3A15; 2–2H3; 1–2A7; 0–0H4; 0–2A1;
4–1H13; 1–1A2; 0–1H11; 0–3A18; 0–3H16; 1–2H13SC;
0–2A8; 3–3H5; 2–1A14; 0–0A6; 1–1H12; 1–3H15;
0–3A3; 2–2H7; 1–2A10; 2–5A4; 1–0H1; 2–2H14;
0–4A17.

HEART OF MIDLOTHIAN (10)

3–2A2SLC; 2–1HSLC; 3–3A12SLC; 0–2H2SLC;
0–4A6SLC; 0–0H12SLC; 3–1A11; 3–1H8; 1–2A2;
1–1H16; 2–1A1; 0–1H4; 3–1A9; 1–3A6; 0–1H12;
2–0H14; 2–4A7; 2–2H17; 2–0A13; 2–3H5; 1–0H15;
3–2A3; 1–1A18; 0–0H11; 2–4A8; 1–1H2; 0–2A16;
3–2H1; 2–1A6SC; 0–5A4; 0–1A12; 0–2A16SC; 1–5A14;
1–0H7; 2–2H6; 1–2A17; 2–2H13; 1–0A5; 2–1H9;
3–0A15; 2–2H3; 2–1H18.

HIBERNIAN (11)

0–1H17SLC; 1–0A15SLC; 2–0H9SLC; 2–2A17SLC;
3–0H15SLC; 2–0A9SLC; 1–3H10; 4–1A27SLC; 0–2A15;
3–2H9; 2–1H27SLC; 1–2A14; 5–1H2; 2–1 6 SLC(SF);
1–1A5; 1–0H12; 1–1H7; 0–3A18; 1–6A16; 5–0H13;
4–3A3; 2–5H4; 6–2A1; 0–0A6; 3–1H8; 0–0A10; 3–0H15;
1–0A9; 1–2H14; 1–3A2; 0–1A16SC; 2–1H5; 1–2A12;
3–0H18; 1–2H16; 3–4A13; 1–2H3; 1–1A4; 1–1H1;
0–3A7; 2–6 4 SLC(F); 1–3H6; 1–2A17; 1–1A8; 4–0H17.

KILMARNOCK (12)

0–4A6SLC; 0–3H2SLC; 3–3H10SLC; 2–2H6SLC;
0–2A2SLC; 0–0A10SLC; 1–1A18; 1–0H13; 3–3A16;
0–1H8; 2–1A3; 3–0H7; 0–1A11; 4–4H15; 1–0A10;
5–1H9; 2–0A14; 1–0H6; 1–2A5; 2–0A2; 2–0H17; 1–1A4;
2–1H1; 0–0H18; 2–3A13; 3–3H16; 1–1A8; 1–0H3;
6–0H Glasgow U. SC; 2–2A7; 1–1A31SC; 4–1H31SC;
2–1H11; 1–0H10; 0–0A15; 0–0A1SC; 0–3H1SC; 1–1H14;
1–1A9; 0–0A6; 0–0H5; 2–1H2; 0–1A17; 1–0A1; 2–2H4.

MORTON (13)

1–3H14SLC; 1–4A4SLC; 0–2A16SLC; 0–2A14SLC;
0–3H4SLC; 0–5H16SLC; 2–0H9; 0–1A12; 5–1H3;
1–0A15; 3–3H14; 2–2A2; 1–2A18; 1–1H4; 3–5A8;
1–0H1; 0–5A11; 0–2A7; 0–2H10; 2–1H6; 0–0A5;
3–2A17; 0–2H16; 1–4A9; 3–2H12; 1–3A3; 3–2H15;
1–2A14; 2–1A9SC; 1–1H2; 3–1A37SC; 0–2H8; 3–2A7SC;
4–3H11; 1–2H7; 3–0H18; 1–4 4 SC(SF); 2–2A10; 2–0A6;
3–6A1; 1–1H5; 4–4H17; 0–3A16; 4–2A4.

PARTICK THISTLE (14)

3–1A13SLC; 1–5H16SLC; 0–4A4SLC; 2–0H13SLC;
1–2A16SLC; 1–6H4SLC; 0–2A16; 4–0H5; 0–1A18;
2–1H11; 3–3A13; 1–0H1; 0–3A15; 2–2A17; 1–1H2;
0–2A10; 0–2H12; 0–4H4; 1–1A6; 0–1H8; 2–2A3; 1–2A7;
0–2H16; 2–1A5; 0–2H18; 2–1A11; 2–1H13; 3–3H4SC;
1–8A4SC; 1–1A1; 2–1H15; 1–2H9; 5–1H10; 1–1A12;
1–2A2; 0–1A4; 0–4H6; 0–2A8; 2–1H3; 1–1H17; 0–0H7;
2–2A9.

RAITH ROVERS (15)

1–1A9SLC; 0–1H11SLC; 0–0A17SLC; 4–2H9SLC;
0–3A11SLC; 2–1H17SLC; 2–3A8; 2–0H11; 2–3A5;
0–1H13; 2–2A18; 3–1H3; 3–0H14; 4–4A12; 1–2A1;
1–2H7; 0–2A4; 3–1H9; 0–3A17; 0–3H16; 0–1A10;
1–2H2; 0–3H8; 0–3A11; 1–1H5; 2–3A13; 0–2H18;
0–2H8SC; 1–0A3; 1–2A14; 0–0H12; 1–3A7; 1–3H4;
3–1A9; 3–2H1; 1–5H17; 2–2A6; 1–2A16; 0–3H10;
0–2A2; 4–0H6.

RANGERS   (16)

0–2H4SLC; 5–1A14SLC; 2–0H13SLC; 0–1A4SLC;
2–1H14SLC; 5–0A13SLC; 2–0H14; 4–2A4; 3–3H12;
1–1A10; 2–1H9; 0–2A17; 3–0H8; 2–3H1; 5–1A3;
6–1H11; 0–1A18; 1–1A5; 1–1H2; 3–0A15; 2–1H7;
2–0A13; 2–0A14; 1–0H4; 3–3A12; 2–0H10; 3–0A9;
1–0H11SC; 3–0H17; 2–0H10SC; 1–0H2SC; 2–1A11;
6–0H18; 2–0H3; 6–0H5; 6–1 1 SC(SF); 2–3A2; 2–1H15;
1–2A7; 0–0A1; 3–0H13; 2–3A6; 0–4 4 SC(F); 1–1H6;
3–0A8.

ST. JOHNSTONE   (17)

1–0A11SLC; 2–3H9SLC; 0–0H15SLC; 2–2H11SLC;
2–2A9SLC; 1–2A15SLC; 1–4H7; 0–2A1; 3–2A6; 0–0H5;
1–3A8; 2–0H16; 1–2A4; 2–2H14; 1–2A9; 2–3H18;
0–3A2; 2–2A10; 3–0H15; 5–1H3; 0–2A12; 2–3H13;
2–4A7; 3–1H1; 3–1H6; 3–0A5; 2–1H8; 3–2H3SC;
0–3A16; 1–1A28SC; 3–0H28SC; 2–3A4SC; 2–1A18;
3–1H2; 2–1H10; 5–1A15; 2–1A3; 2–3H4; 1–0H12;
1–1A14; 4–4A13; 2–1H11; 4–0H9; 0–4A11.

ST. MIRREN   (18)

2–1A31SLC; 3–0H30SLC; 0–6A32SLC; 1–0H31SLC;
1–2A30SLC; 2–0H32SLC; 1–1H12; 1–1A3; 1–0H14;
2–0A9; 2–2H15; 0–0A6; 2–1H13; 1–1A2; 3–0H11;
3–2A17; 1–0H16; 0–2A1; 1–1H7; 0–5A4; 2–6A8; 1–0H5;
1–1H10; 0–0A12; 2–1H3; 2–0A14; 3–0H9; 2–0A15;
1–0A26SC; 2–3H6; 1–1A2SC; 1–2H2; 1–3H2SC;
0–3A11; 1–2H17; 0–6A16; 1–2H1; 0–3A13; 2–2A7;
0–3H4; 1–2H8; 0–0A5; 1–2A10.

DIVISION TWO

ALBION ROVERS (19)

4–0A26SLC; 3–2H34SLC; 2–4H29SLC; 0–7A32;
5–0H26SLC; 3–2A34SLC; 2–2A29SLC; 3–3A37SLC;
0–2H37SLC; 5–3A30; 3–1A31; 2–1H29; 5–4H31;
4–1A23; 2–0A25; 0–0H34; 1–3A26; 1–1H37; 3–2A35;
2–1H28; 1–0H33; 2–1A20; 1–1A36; 3–1H24; 0–0A22;
4–1H27; 0–3A21; 5–0H30; 1–4A29; 0–1A35SC; 1–0H25;
1–1A34; 2–1H23; 1–2H26; 0–3A33; 2–0H20; 2–1H36;
0–2A24; 2–1H22; 0–2A27; 0–3A37; 0–1H21; 0–1A28;
4–2H35; 0–1H32.

ALLOA ATHLETIC (20)

0–1H35SLC; 3–2A23SLC; 0–3A21; 2–2A28SLC;
0–1H37SLC; 1–2H21; 4–4A35; 1–0H22; 0–2H37;
2–3A22; 1–1A29; 2–0H23; 2–0A24; 0–2H32; 2–3A30;
1–2H36; 1–2A31; 1–2H19; 1–5A28; 0–1H25; 1–4A26;
6–1H Ross Co. SC; 0–3A33; 0–5A27; 4–4H35; 1–1A37;
0–0H28SC; 1–2A28SC; 3–1A23; 3–3H24; 0–3H29;
0–4A32; 0–4A34; 1–1A36; 1–2H31; 0–2A19; 2–0H28;
3–2A25; 0–1H26; 1–2H33; 2–2H34; 1–2H27; 3–1H30.

AYR UNITED (21)

3–1H25SLC; 4–2A36SLC; 1–1A3SLC; 3–0H20;
2–0A25SLC; 1–0H36SLC; 3–1H3SLC; 2–1A20;
0–1H5SLC; 2–0A31; 1–4A32; 1–5H34; 0–2A5SLC;
1–1A22; 2–2H33; 1–1A25; 7–1H35; 0–1A27; 4–1H29;
3–0A26; 1–2H36; 2–0A37; 6–1H28; 1–0H30; 6–1H23;
3–0H19; 4–0H31; 3–0A34; 2–0H22; 1–0H33SC; 4–0H25;
2–6A7SC; 2–1H27; 4–0H26; 0–0A36; 3–0H37; 1–2A28;
2–2A30; 0–0H24; 2–1A35; 3–0A23; 1–0A19; 1–1H32;
2–3A33; 1–0A24; 1–0A29.

194

BERWICK RANGERS (22)

1–1H33SLC; 4–2A24SLC; 0–1A27SLC; 0–1A33;
0–2A33SLC; 3–0H24SLC; 1–4H27SLC; 0–2H33;
3–728; 0–1A20; 2–0H27; 3–2H20; 1–1A24; 1–1H21;
1–2A23; 0–1H36; 2–0H26; 0–2A37; 0–0H30; 1–7A32;
3–1H31; 3–1A35; 1–1A25; 0–0H19; 1–3A34; 3–0H28;
1–4A27; 2–0A Nairn Co. SC; 0–2A21; 0–0H23;
0–3A1SC; 1–3A36; 1–3A26; 1–5H37; 1–3H32; 0–1A31;
2–4H35; 0–4H25; 1–2A19; 0–2A30; 1–1H34; 0–0H29;
3–3A29; 5–0H24.

BRECHIN CITY (23)

2–3H20SLC; 2–1A37SLC; 3–1H24; 0–1A35SLC;
3–0H28SLC; 0–0A24; 2–1H31; 0–2H30; 1–4H19;
0–2A20; 2–1H22; 1–3A37; 0–2H36; 1–2A26; 5–1H25;
1–2A35; 1–2H28; 0–3H29; 0–2A32; 4–1H34; 1–1H31SC;
2–3A31SC; 1–6A21; 1–3H20; 0–0A22; 1–2A19; 0–1H37;
0–3A36; 4–4H35; 1–0A28; 1–2A34; 0–0H32; 1–6A27;
1–6A31; 0–3H27; 1–0H26; 0–3H21; 0–3A25; 2–1A33;
1–1H33; 3–3A29; 1–2A30.

CLYDEBANK (24)

0–2A27SLC; 2–4H22SLC; 2–1A33SLC; 1–3A23;
1–3H27SLC; 0–3A22SLC; 1–1H33SLC; 0–0H23;
0–1H26; 3–3A25; 4–2A34; 1–1H25; 1–1H22; 1–1A33;
0–2H20; 2–1A30; 0–4H28; 3–5A31; 2–2H37; 0–4H32;
1–4H27; 1–3A19; 0–0A35; 0–1A25SC; 0–2A36; 3–3A26;
1–3H34; 3–0H29; 3–3H33; 3–3A20; 5–0H31; 1–1A37;
5–0H30; 1–2A32; 1–1A27; 2–0H19; 2–2H35; 0–0A21;
0–1A29; 0–1A28; 2–2H36; 0–5A22; 0–1H21.

COWDENBEATH   (25)

1–3A21SLC; 1–1H3SLC; 1–2A36SLC; 1–2A36;
0–2H21SLC; 0–2A3SLC; 3–6H36SLC; 0–1H36; 0–1A27;
3–3H24; 1–3H28; 1–1A24; 1–0A37; 0–2H19; 1–4A32;
1–1H21; 1–3H29; 1–5A23; 3–2H34; 0–4A33; 3–1H26;
1–0A20; 1–1H22; 1–0H24SC; 1–2H30; 3–1A35; 0–1A28;
2–0A30SC; 0–1A19; 0–5H32; 0–1A31SC; 0–4A21;
3–1A29; 1–0A34; 1–2H33; 3–0A26; 2–3H20; 4–0A22;
2–3H31; 0–4H27; 2–2A30; 3–0H23; 6–0H35; 4–1H37;
0–3A31.

DUMBARTON   (26)

0–4H19SLC; 0–1A29SLC; 4–3H34SLC; 1–2H31;
0–5A19SLC; 5–1H29SLC; 0–1A34SLC; 0–2A31;
1–0A24; 1–3H36; 1–1A27; 1–4A28; 1–3H37; 2–3A35;
3–1H19; 0–2A22; 2–1H23; 1–4A33; 0–3H21; 0–2A29;
1–3A25; 1–0H30; 4–1H20; 1–1H27; 1–1A32; 0–2H34;
3–3H24; 0–3A36; 3–2H Vale of Leithen SC; 2–1A37;
5–1H35; 0–1H18SC; 2–1A19; 3–1H22; 0–2H33; 0–4A21;
2–3H29; 0–3H25; 0–0A30; 1–0A20; 0–1A23; 2–4H32;
0–2A34; 4–1H28.

EAST FIFE   (27)

2–0H24SLC; 1–1A33SLC; 1–0H22SLC; 0–0H34;
3–1A24SLC; 1–1H33SLC; 4–1A22SLC; 2–0A34;
1–0H25; 1–4H11SLC; 0–2A22; 1–1H26; 1–1H33;
1–2A11SLC; 1–0A30; 1–2H29; 0–4A32; 1–0H21;
6–1H31; 2–1A36; 2–1H37; 4–1A24; 5–0H35; 0–3A28;
1–1A26; 1–4A19; 5–0H20; 4–1H22; 2–4A33; 5–0H30;
1–3A37SC; 3–1H32; 1–2A21; 1–3A31; 3–2H36; 1–1A37;
1–1H24; 4–1A35; 6–1H23; 4–2H28; 3–0A23; 4–0A25;
2–0H19; 2–1A20; 2–3A29.

EAST STIRLING (28)

1–2A37SLC; 3–0H35SLC; 2–2H37; 2–2H20SLC;
0–3A23SLC; 7–3H22; 6–0H35; 3–1A25; 2–0A35;
4–1H26; 5–1H31; 2–3A34; 4–0A24; 0–1H33; 1–2A19;
2–4H29; 2–1A23; 5–1H20; 1–6A21; 3–0H27; 0–0A30;
0–1H36; 0–4H32; 0–3A22; 1–0H25; 0–0A20SC;
2–1H20SC; 2–2A31; 2–0H36SC; 2–1H34; 1–1H17SC;
0–3A17SC; 4–2A29; 0–1H23; 0–2A20; 2–1H21; 2–4A27;
3–3A33; 1–0H30; 1–1A36; 1–0H24; 0–4A32; 1–0H19;
1–4A26; 0–3A37.

FORFAR ATHLETIC (29)

0–4A34SLC; 1–0H26SLC; 4–2A19SLC; 1–1H30;
0–2H34SLC; 1–5A26SLC; 2–2H19SLC; 3–1A30;
1–0H32; 1–2A19; 1–1H20; 3–2H36; 2–1A27; 9–1H35;
3–1A25; 1–2H34; 1–4A21; 4–2A28; 2–0H26; 3–0A23;
3–1H31; 3–1H37; 1–2H Nairn Co. SC; 1–3A32;
4–1H19; 0–3A24; 1–2A36; 3–0A20; 2–1A35; 1–3H25;
2–2A34; 2–4H28; 3–2A26; 0–0A31; 0–1A37; 1–0H33;
1–0H24; 0–5A33; 0–0A22; 3–3H22; 3–2H27; 3–3H23;
0–1H21.

HAMILTON ACADEMICALS (30)

2–1H32SLC; 0–3A18SLC; 2–0A31SLC; 1–1A29;
0–0A32SLC; 2–1H18SLC; 2–0H31SLC; 1–3H29;
3–5H19; 0–10A4SLC; 1–2A32; 2–0A23; 4–4H31;
2–4H4SLC; 0–1H27; 1–7A36; 1–2H24; 2–1A33; 3–2H20;
0–0A22; 0–1A37; 2–1H35; 0–2H34; 0–1A26; 0–1A21;
0–0H28; 2–1A25; 0–5A19; 0–1H32; 0–2H25SC; 0–5A27;
1–1H36; 0–3H33; 0–5A24; 1–3H37; 0–1A34; 1–3A35;
0–0H26; 2–2H21; 0–1A28; 2–0H22; 2–2H25; 2–1A31;
1–3A20; 2–1H23.

MONTROSE (31)

1–2H18SLC; 2–1A32SLC; 0–2H30SLC; 2–1A26;
0–1A18SLC; 2–1H32SLC; 0–2A30SLC; 2–0H26;
1–2A23; 1–3H19; 0–2H21; 4–5A19; 4–4A30; 3–0H35;
1–5A28; 1–0H33; 0–1A34; 5–3H24; 1–6A27; 2–1H20;
1–3A22; 0–2H32; 1–3A29; 0–2A36; 1–1A23SC;
3–2H23SC; 1–0A37; 0–4A21; 6–1H Fraserburgh SC;
2–2A35; 2–2H28; 1–0H25SC; 0–1A33; 1–1H12SC;
1–4A12SC; 0–5A24; 3–1H27; 2–1A20; 1–0H22; 1–4A32;
0–0H29; 0–2H36; 6–1H23; 3–2A25; 1–2H30; 2–0H37;
3–1H34; 3–0H25.

MOTHERWELL (32)

1–2A30SLC; 1–2H31SLC; 6–0H18SLC; 7–0H19;
0–0H30SLC; 1–2A31SLC; 0–2A18SLC; 0–1A29;
2–1H30; 4–1H21; 6–1A35; 2–1A34; 4–1H25; 2–0A20;
4–0H27; 4–0A36; 7–1H22; 4–0A24; 2–0A31; 2–0H23;
2–2H33; 2–0A37; 1–1H26; 4–0A28; 3–1H29; 1–0A30;
5–1H34; 5–0A25; 1–1H5SC; 1–2A5SC; 4–0H20; 1–3A27;
3–1A22; 2–1H24; 4–1H31; 0–0A23; 2–1A33; 3–0H37;
4–2A26; 7–1H35; 4–0H28; 1–1A21; 3–0H36; 1–0A19.

QUEEN OF THE SOUTH (33)

1–1A22SLC; 1–1H27SLC; 1–2H24SLC; 1–0H22;
2–0H22SLC; 1–1A27SLC; 1–1A24SLC; 2–0A22;
0–2A37; 3–1H34; 5–1H35; 4–0A34; 1–1A27; 1–1H24;
2–2A21; 0–1A31; 1–2H30; 1–0A28; 4–1H26; 0–1A19;
4–0H25; 0–1H36; 2–2A32; 3–0H20; 0–2H37; 4–3A35;
4–2H27; 3–3A24; 0–1A21SC; 1–0H31; 3–0A30; 2–0A26;
3–0H19; 2–1A25; 3–2A36; 1–2H32; 3–3H28; 0–1A29;
2–1A20; 5–0H29; 1–2H23; 1–1A23; 3–2H21.

QUEEN'S PARK (34)

4–0H29SLC; 2–3A19SLC; 3–4A26SLC; 0–0A27;
2–0A29SLC; 2–3H19SLC; 1–0H26SLC; 0–2H27;
0–3A36; 1–3A33; 2–4H24; 0–4H33; 5–1A21; 1–2H32;
0–0A19; 3–2H28; 1–0H31; 2–1A29; 2–0H35; 2–3A25;
2–0A30; 1–1H37; 1–4A23; 3–1H22; 2–0A26; 0–2H36;
3–1A24; 0–3H21; 1–5A32; 1–1H19; 1–2A7SC; 1–2A28;
4–0H20; 2–2H29; 0–1H25; 1–0H30; 2–1H23; 0–2A37;
1–1A22; 2–2A20; 2–0H26; 1–2A35; 1–3A31.

STENHOUSEMUIR (35)

1–0A20SLC; 1–3H37SLC; 0–3A28SLC; 1–0H23SLC;
4–4H20; 0–6A28; 1–5A33; 0–2H28; 1–6H32; 0–3A31;
3–2H26; 1–9A29; 1–7A21; 2–3H19; 0–2A34; 2–1H23;
1–2A30; 1–3H22; 0–5A27; 0 0H24; 1–5A36; 1–2II37;
1–3H25; 4–4A20; 3–4H33; 1–0H19SC; 2–2H31; 1–5A26;
0–3H2SC; 1–2H29; 4–4A23; 3–1H30; 4–2A22; 1–4H27;
2–2A24; 2–0H36; 1–2H21; 2–5A37; 1–7A32; 0–6A25;
2–1H34; 2–4A19.

STIRLING ALBION (36)

1–2A3SLC; 2–4H21SLC; 2–1H25SLC; 2–1H25;
1–0H3SLC; 0–1A21SLC; 6–3A25SLC; 1–0A25; 3–0H34;
3–1A26; 3–2H37; 2–3A29; 7–1H30; 1–0A22; 2–0A23;
0–4H32; 2–1A20; 1–2H27; 2–1A21; 1–1H19; 1–0A33;
2–0H31; 5–1H35; 1–0A28; 2–0H24; 2–0A34; 3–0H26;
2–1H29; 1–1A30; 0–2A28SC; 3–1H22; 3–0H23; 1–1H20;
2–3A27; 0–0H21; 1–2A19; 2–3H33; 2–0A31; 0–2A35;
1–1H28; 2–2A24; 1–2A37; 0–3A32.

STRANRAER (37)

2–1H28SLC; 3–1A35SLC; 1–2H23SLC; 2–2A28;
1–0A20SLC; 3–3H19SLC; 2–0A19SLC; 2–0H33;
0–4H6SLC; 2–0A20; 2–3A36; 0–1H25; 0–6A6SLC;
3–1A26; 3–1H23; 1–1A19; 2–0H22; 2–2A24; 1–0H30;
1–2A27; 0–2H21; 1–1A34; 1–3A29; 0–2H32; 2–1A35;
0–1H31; 2–0A33; 1–1H20; 2–0H Elgin C. SC; 1–2H26;
3–1H27SC; 1–0A23; 1–3H13SC; 5–1A22; 1–1H24;
3–1A30; 1–1H27; 0–3A21; 2–0H34; 1–0H29; 0–3A32;
5–2H35; 3–0H19; 0–2A31; 2–1H36; 1–4A25; 3–0H28.

*The man with spring in his heels and sting in his head: Alan
Gilzean leaps for the ball in the Scotland versus West
Germany game.'Keeper Wolter punches clear as Schnellinger
covers up*

Week-by-week League positions last season

Division 1

ABERDEEN
5 8 11 14 16 16 16 14 14 15 13 14 15 16 13 13 14 14
15 15 15 15 15 15 15 15 15 15 15 15 15 15

AIRDRIEONIANS
8 5 10 12 14 15 15 15 15 12 14 11 13 12 11 10 10 10
9 9 9 8 8 8 8 7 7 7 9 8 8 8 7

ARBROATH
15 18 18 18 18 18 18 18 18 18 18 18 18 18 18 18 18
18 18 18 18 18 18 18 18 18 17 18 18 18 18 18

CELTIC
10 9 6 5 1 1 1 1 1 1 1 1 1 1 1 1 1 1 1 1 1 1 1 1 1 1 1 1
1 1 1 1 1 1

CLYDE
18 16 14 10 10 9 6 7 7 8 7 7 7 6 8 8 9 11 11 11 12
12 12 13 13 12 9 13 12 12 11 11 13

DUNDEE
14 17 12 13 15 13 11 12 10 7 9 9 10 10 12 12 13 13 13
12 10 10 10 11 14 11 10 12 13 11 12 10 9

DUNDEE UNITED
1 1 1 1 6 4 3 3 3 3 2 2 2 3 2 2 2 3 5 6 6 5 6 5 5 5 5
5 5 4 5 5

DUNFERMLINE
12 10 7 7 2 6 4 4 6 5 5 4 3 2 4 4 4 4 6 4 4 3 3 3 4 4
4 4 3 3 3 3

FALKIRK
13 13 17 17 17 17 17 17 17 17 17 17 17 17 17 17 17
17 17 17 17 17 17 17 17 17 18 17 17 17 17 17

HEARTS
2 4 5 6 8 5 8 9 8 9 8 8 8 8 7 7 8 8 7 8 8 9 9 9 9 9 12
9 6 6 6 7 8

HIBERNIAN
16 14 16 11 12 11 12 13 13 11 10 10 9 9 9 9 7 7 8 7
7 7 7 7 7 8 11 10 11 13 13 13 12

KILMARNOCK
4 7 9 8 5 8 9 6 5 4 3 5 4 4 3 3 5 6 4 3 3 4 2 2 3 3 3
3 4 5 4 4

MORTON
6 3 2 3 3 7 7 8 9 10 11 12 11 11 10 11 11 9 10 10 11
11 11 12 12 14 13 11 10 10 10 12 10

PARTICK THISTLE
7 11 8 9 9 12 13 10 11 13 15 15 16 14 15 15 15 15 14
14 14 13 13 10 11 13 14 14 14 14 14 14

203

RAITH ROVERS

9 12 15 15 11 10 10 11 12 14 12 13 14 15 16 16 16 16
16 16 16 16 16 16 16 16 16 16 16 16 16 16

RANGERS

3 2 4 2 7 3 5 5 4 6 6 6 5 5 5 5 3 2 2 2 2 2 4 4 2 2 2
2 2 2 2 2

ST. JOHNSTONE

17 15 13 16 13 14 14 16 16 16 16 16 12 13 14 14 12
12 12 13 13 14 14 14 10 10 8 8 7 7 7 6

ST. MIRREN

11 6 3 4 4 2 2 2 2 2 2 4 3 6 7 6 6 6 5 3 5 5 6 5 6 6 6
6 6 8 9 9 9 11

Division 2

ALBION ROVERS

11 5 4 2 3 5 5 5 3 3 2 2 2 2 3 3 3 3 3 3 3 3 3 3 4 4 5
5 4 5 6 5 6 6 6 7

ALLOA ATHLETIC

14 13 16 12 9 12 12 13 16 16 16 17 18 18 18 18 18 18
17 17 17 17 17 17 17 17 18 16 16 15 15 17 18 17 18

AYR UNITED

5 4 9 11 8 9 7 8 8 8 9 8 7 6 7 5 4 4 4 4 4 4 4 3 3 3
3 3 3 3 3 2 2

BERWICK RANGERS

18 14 13 13 14 14 13 15 15 15 13 12 12 11 11 11 12
11 11 12 12 12 12 14 15 15 15 15 15 16 16 16 16 15
16

BRECHIN CITY

3 7 12 14 13 13 15 17 13 13 15 15 16 14 16 16 16 17
18 18 18 18 18 18 18 18 16 17 17 18 18 18 17 18 17

CLYDEBANK

16 11 8 10 12 10 11 12 12 12 14 14 15 17 17 17 17 14
14 14 14 14 14 12 12 12 13 12 11 11 12 12 12 13

COWDENBEATH

19 17 15 16 17 17 18 18 18 17 18 16 14 13 15 15 14
13 15 16 16 16 15 15 15 14 14 14 14 14 14 14 13 12

DUMBARTON

12 15 18 18 18 16 17 16 17 18 17 18 17 16 14 14 15
16 13 11 11 11 11 11 11 11 12 13 13 12 13 13 14 14

EAST FIFE

2 8 6 6 7 8 10 10 9 9 7 7 5 7 6 8 6 7 5 5 6 7 6 7 7 6
6 6 6 4 4 4 3 3

EAST STIRLING

9 3 1 3 1 3 3 4 5 6 6 6 8 5 5 7 8 8 8 8 8 8 8 8 8 8
8 8 9 8 8 9 9

FORFAR ATHLETIC

4 9 7 7 6 6 4 6 6 5 5 4 4 4 4 4 5 6 7 7 5 5 7 6 6 7 7
7 7 7 7 7 7 7 6

HAMILTON ACADEMICALS

15 16 14 15 15 18 16 14 14 14 12 13 13 15 13 12 13
15 16 15 15 15 16 16 16 16 17 18 18 17 17 15 15 16
15

MONTROSE

6 12 11 9 11 11 9 9 11 10 10 11 11 12 12 13 11 12 12
13 13 13 13 14 13 13 11 11 12 13 11 11 11 11 10

MOTHERWELL

10 10 5 4 4 1 1 1 1 1 1 1 1 1 1 1 1 1 1 1 1 1 1 1 2 1
1 1 1 1 1 1 1 1

QUEEN OF THE SOUTH

7 2 2 1 2 4 6 5 4 4 4 5 6 8 8 6 7 5 6 6 7 6 5 5 5 4 4
5 4 5 6 5 5 5

QUEEN'S PARK

17 19 17 17 16 15 14 11 10 11 11 10 10 10 10 10 9 10
10 9 9 10 9 10 10 10 10 10 10 10 10 10 10 10 11

STENHOUSEMUIR

13 18 19 19 19 19 19 19 19 19 19 19 19 19 19 19 19
19 19 19 19 19 19 19 19 19 19 19 19 19 19 19 19 19

STIRLING ALBION

1 1 3 5 5 2 2 2 2 3 3 3 3 2 2 2 2 2 2 2 2 2 2 2 1 2 2
2 2 2 2 2 4 4

STRANRAER

8 6 10 8 10 7 8 7 7 7 8 9 9 9 9 9 10 9 9 10 10 9 10
9 9 9 9 9 9 8 9 9 8 8

HERE'S MUD IN YOUR EYE

It's all part of the game ... Clyde goalie John Wright after a nose-dive into the mire at Shawfield in a match against Dundee